MACBETH

MACBETH

William Shakespeare

Series Editor: Jane Bachman

Consulting Editor: Skip Nicholson

NTC *Publishing Group*
a division of NTC/CONTEMPORARY PUBLISHING COMPANY
Lincolnwood, Illinois USA

Interior illustrations: Diane Novario

Cover illustration from the Art Collection of the Folger Shakespeare Library.

ISBN: 0-8442-5737-0

Published by NTC Publishing Group,
a division of NTC/Contemporary Publishing Company,
4255 West Touhy Avenue,
Lincolnwood (Chicago), Illinois 60646-1975 U.S.A.
© 1994 by NTC/Contemporary Publishing Company
Manufactured in the United States of America.
Library of Congress Catalog Card Number: 92-60872

8 9 0 VP 9 8 7 6 5 4

CONTENTS

Introducing Shakespeare

Most of what we know about William Shakespeare's life is based only on public records or on allusions to his work in various letters and diaries of his day. He was baptized on April 26, 1564, in Trinity Church in Stratford-upon-Avon and buried there on April 25, 1616. His birthday is usually celebrated on April 23, also the date of his death.

Stratford is in Warwickshire, a county northwest of London. In Shakespeare's time it was a small market town. His father, John Shakespeare, was a prosperous townsman who made gloves and was also a tanner as well as a dealer in farm produce. John Shakespeare held various town offices. However, in 1586 he was forced into bankruptcy because he could not pay his debts. Mary Arden, Shakespeare's mother, was the daughter of Robert Arden, a well-to-do farmer who left her money and a small estate in addition to several properties he had given her before his death. For most of their life together, the parents of William Shakespeare were reasonably well off.

William Shakespeare was the third of eight children, two of whom died before his birth and one of whom died when William was a boy. Only a sister, Joan, survived him; one of his brothers, Edmund, may have been an actor.

Shakespeare probably attended the grammar school in Stratford, where he might have learned Latin and Greek. Records show that he married Anne Hathaway, eight years his senior, in Stratford in 1582. He and Anne had three children: Susanna, born in 1583, and twins Judith and Hamnet, born in 1585. Hamnet died at the age of eleven.

The next record of Shakespeare is in 1592, when he was evidently in London. In the pamphlet *A Groatsworth of Wit*, addressed to fellow playwrights who were university graduates (as Shakespeare was not), Robert Greene bitterly refers to Shakespeare as "an upstart crow, beautified with our feathers, that with his Tyger's hart wrapt in a Player's hyde supposes he is as well able to bombast out a blanke verse as the best of you; and being an absolute *Johannes fac totum*, is in his owne conceit the only Shake-scene in a country." The phrase "Tyger's hart" refers to a line in *Henry VI, Part 3* by Shakespeare, a play probably first produced in 1591. *Johannes fac totum* means "jack-of-all-trades." Some scholars think that Shakespeare began his career as an actor, probably sometime before 1592, and that when he began to write plays, he angered many established playwrights, such as Greene.

Although the date of Shakespeare's arrival in London is not certain, it is known that some of his early plays were produced by an acting company known as Lord Pembroke's Men. He might have acted with this company as well. In 1594 he became a member of a company called Lord

Chamberlain's Men, for which he wrote many successful plays, and in 1599 he became a partner in the newly constructed Globe Theatre. This partnership assured his financial success and enabled him to invest in considerable property, both in Stratford and in London.

Shakespeare early achieved recognition as a poet, and in 1598 one writer referred to him as "mellifluous and honey-tongued" when writing of Shakespeare's long poem *Venus and Adonis*, first published in 1593. All in all, some 37 plays and 154 sonnets are attributed to Shakespeare.

Critics sometimes divide his dramatic career into four periods: the Early Period (1564–1594); the Period of Comedies and Histories (1595–1601); the Period of Tragedies (1602–1608); and the Period of Romances (1609–1616). The first attempt at publishing a collection of his plays was in 1623, when the First Folio was published. (The printer's term *folio* refers to the folding of the printed sheets.) The First Folio contains thirty-six plays. A later play, *Pericles*, was added to the second edition of the Third Folio in 1664. During his life, however, eighteen of Shakespeare's plays were published in quarto editions. (Again a printer's term, a *quarto* was a smaller, squarer book than a folio.)

In 1611 or 1612 Shakespeare returned permanently to Stratford where he wrote his last plays. The cause of Shakespeare's death at age fifty-two is unknown. His wife and both daughters survived him and are mentioned in his will, which also mentions small bequests to various friends and to the poor of Stratford.

Introducing *Macbeth*

Macbeth has been a favorite of readers, theatre-goers, and actors for almost four hundred years and is considered one of the best of Shakespeare's plays. First of all, it tells a good story—a story of ambition, murder, and madness, all quite enough to keep readers or audience entertained and to provide an irresistible challenge to actors. Second, it represents Shakespeare at the height of his dramatic powers. One critic has called the plot "perfectly unified."

Did Shakespeare devise the plot? Yes and no. Even in Shakespeare's time, the adage that there are no new plots was true. In fact, he took some of the story from history, added his own embellishments, and shaped the whole into an imaginative work that was uniquely his own.

Shakespeare was alive when Raphael Holinshed (hol'ən shed) published his *Chronicles* in 1577 (revised 1587). The *Chronicles* are an account of British history. They contain accounts of ancient Scottish royalty and describe supernatural happenings, supposedly foreshadowing bloody events in various struggles for power. Shakespeare combined several stories about eleventh-century people and events to shape the plot and characters of *Macbeth*. But Shakespeare was not writing history. He was merely using it. It might be more accurate to say that history provided him with ideas about human nature, politics, and destiny.

Macbeth is a tragedy, one of eleven that Shakespeare wrote. Like other tragedies, this one centers on a prominent person who, after a significant struggle, suffers defeat. In this defeat the person achieves heroic stature.

Macbeth was probably written in 1606, shortly after James I succeeded Elizabeth I to the English throne. Many scholars think that Shakespeare wrote the play for presentation before James because the play reflects so many of James's interests. James was Scottish (he was also known as James VI of Scotland), and he claimed descent from Banquo, a character in the play. (Modern scholars now know that Banquo is entirely legendary, however.) James wrote a book called *Demonologie*, in which he speculated about the nature and practice of witches. No one knows whether Shakespeare believed in witches or simply used them to create atmosphere in the play. Still, one can speculate that the opening scene of *Macbeth* must have focused James's attention immediately, as it does theatre audiences today.

A Note on Shakespeare's Language

BLANK VERSE

Your face, my thane, is as a book where men
May read strange matters. To beguile the time,
Look like the time; bear welcome in your eye . . .

In order to read Lady Macbeth's lines so that they make sense, you can read according to the punctuation, pausing only at commas and stopping only at the period and semicolon. There is a rhythm to these lines, however. Notice that as you read the first line aloud, your emphasis naturally and lightly falls on five words:

Your fáce | my tháne | is aś | a boók | where mén

Because there are five stressed words in this line, the rhythm, or *meter*, is called *pentameter* (*penta* means five). Each marked-off division is called a *foot*. A foot of two syllables, the first unstressed, the second stressed, is called an *iamb*. Thus, the line above is described as *iambic pentameter*.

This pattern of an unaccented syllable followed by an accented syllable is natural to much English speech and poetry, some of it rhymed, some of it unrhymed. Notice the iambic meter in the first part of the song "America":

Ŏ beaútiful fŏr spácĭous skíes

Shakespeare is writing verse throughout most of *Macbeth*, but it is unrhymed verse or *blank verse*, which is iambic pentameter that does not rhyme.

WORD ORDER

Often in Shakespeare's lines, the words are not in the order you are accustomed to. Putting the words in their usual order may help make meaning more clear.

Shakespeare's order	Usual order
Dismayed not this our captains?	Did not this dismay our captains?
	or
	Weren't our captains dismayed by this?
So foul and fair a day I have not seen.	I have not seen so foul and fair a day.

As you read the play, use this technique to unravel the meanings of lines with words that seem reversed or out of normal order.

FIGURATIVE LANGUAGE

One of the things that makes Shakespeare so quotable is his use of figurative language. Sleep is not just good for you, it "knits up the raveled sleave of care." The sun is not just eclipsed, but "dark night strangles the traveling lamp."

In both examples, Shakespeare has used *personification*, a figure of speech in which an inanimate object or a quality is made to seem alive, to have human characteristics: Sleep "knits up" and dark night "strangles." But in both lines, he has also used *metaphor*, another kind of figurative language. "Care," or everyday concern, is compared to a tangled thread(sleave) that is untangled or knitted up, just as a day's cares are banished by sleep. The "traveling lamp" is the sun, which seems to move across the sky.

Shakespeare's use of figurative language delights readers by letting them experience things in new ways. As you read, decide whether a passage that seems puzzling contains figurative, not literal, language, and you may be better able to decipher meaning.

Introducing the Globe Theatre

The Globe is the sixteenth-century theatre most closely associated with Shakespeare, for he had a financial interest in it, acted there, and wrote many of his plays for the actors at the Globe.

James Burbage built the first theatre in London, known simply as the Theatre, in 1576. In 1599 the Theatre was dismantled by Burbage's two sons, Richard and Cuthbert, and rebuilt as the Globe on the opposite side of the Thames River. Richard and Cuthbert Burbage held a half interest in the Globe, and five actors divided the other half interest, among them Shakespeare.

The Globe burned in 1613 when, during a performance of Shakespeare's *Henry VIII*, a cannon discharged backstage and touched off a fire in the thatched roof. The Globe was rebuilt on the same site, and we know something about its features from the surviving specifications for another theatre.

In 1600 Philip Henslowe built the Fortune theatre, and the contractor was directed to build the Fortune like the Globe, with at least one exception: it was to be square instead of polygonal.

There are a few other clues about the appearance of the Globe. Several period drawings and engravings of London and of theatres, including the Globe, still exist. Perhaps the most interesting recent event was the 1989 discovery and excavation of the remains of the Rose Theatre, built in London in 1586 quite near the Globe.

Suppose for a moment that you are a playgoer. It is early afternoon and you have reached the Globe on foot, or you have been rowed in a ferry across the Thames from the north side. As you approach the theatre, you see a flag flying from the top to indicate that a performance will be given today. Since the theatre holds 2,000 to 3,000 people, and most Londoners are avid playgoers, you soon find yourself in the midst of a huge throng.

When you enter the theatre, you can look up at the sky, for the circular area, or pit, in front of the stage is not roofed. Turning, you note that there are three levels of spectator's galleries on three sides of the theatre and a gallery above and at the back of the stage as well.

The floor of the theatre is about 5 ½ feet below the stage and about 70 feet in diameter. If you have only a penny to spend, this is where you will stand, elbow to elbow with other spectators, to see the performance. If you can afford more, you will ascend the stairs to one of the galleries, where you will be able to sit protected from the weather.

The stage itself is a little over forty feet wide and about twenty-seven feet deep. You have heard that the floor of the stage contains a trap door, a convenient opening for the emergence of special effects such as smoke.

At the back of the stage are two (possibly three) doors, which open inward and may be covered by curtains. The actors will appear through these doors from the tiring house, or dressing rooms, behind the stage. The central area behind the curtains may be used as a small "discovery space" for some plays. In a performance of *Hamlet*, for example, Polonius hides behind the curtain before he is stabbed.

If the gallery above and at the back of the stage is needed for the performance, there will be no spectators there. In *Romeo and Juliet*, this area represents Juliet's window, where she stands to speak to Romeo below.

The roof above the stage is decorated and is supported by at least two pillars. Above the roof is an area that probably contains ropes and pulleys for lowering and raising actors and props.

The stage itself has few props and no scenery. There may be a throne for a king, a curtained bed for Juliet, a few stools and tables for interior scenes, and candles or torches to indicate night. Exterior scenes are indicated by the actors' speeches, as in *A Midsummer Night's Dream* when Quince says, "Here's a marvelous place for our rehearsal. This green plot shall be our stage, this hawthorn brake our tiring-house." There are costumes, however, which are the property of the acting company and are not to be worn by the actors when they are not performing.

Such simple equipment enables the acting companies to pack up and tour the countryside when, on occasion, the London theatres are closed because of an outbreak of the plague.

For the moment, however, the day is warm and sunny, and the Globe is filled with an enthusiastic and noisy crowd. Your fellow "groundlings" you notice, reek somewhat of garlic, may not have had a bath recently, and tend to jostle you as they try to find a good viewing spot. But the noise lessens and you forget your surroundings as the first actor steps onto the stage.

CHARACTERS

DUNCAN, *King of Scotland*

MALCOLM ⎫
            ⎬ *his sons*
DONALBAIN ⎭

MACBETH, *Thane of Glamis and
    Cawdor; later King of Scotland*

LADY MACBETH, *Macbeth's wife*

BANQUO, *a thane of Scotland*

FLEANCE, *Banquo's son*

MACDUFF, *Thane of Fife*

LADY MACDUFF, *Macduff's wife*

SON *of Macduff and Lady Macduff*

LENNOX ⎫
ROSS ⎪
      ⎬ *noblemen and thanes
MENTEITH ⎪ of Scotland*
ANGUS ⎪
CAITHNESS ⎭

SIWARD, *Earl of Northumberland*

YOUNG SIWARD, *his son*

SEYTON, *an officer attending Macbeth*

ENGLISH DOCTOR

SCOTTISH DOCTOR

GENTLEWOMAN *attending Lady
    Macbeth*

SERGEANT

PORTER

OLD MAN

THREE MURDERERS

THREE WITCHES

HECATE

THREE APPARITIONS

LORDS, GENTLEMEN, OFFICERS,
    SOLDIERS, MESSENGERS,
    SERVANTS, *and* ATTENDANTS

SCENE: *Scotland; England.*

ACT I

"When shall we three meet again?
In thunder, lightning, or in rain?"

5 **ere** (ār) before.

8 **Graymalkin** gray cat, the first witch's *familiar*, or evil spirit who acts as a servant, here in the likeness of a cat.

9 **Paddock** toad, the second witch's familiar.

s.d.* **Exeunt** (ek'si ənt) they go off.

*stage directions

SCENE 1

The witches gather and prepare to meet Macbeth.

A deserted place.

Thunder and lightning. Enter three WITCHES.

FIRST WITCH.   When shall we three meet again
  In thunder, lightning, or in rain?

SECOND WITCH.   When the hurlyburly's done,
  When the battle's lost and won.

THIRD WITCH.   That will be ere the set of sun.   5

FIRST WITCH.   Where the place?

SECOND WITCH.   Upon the heath.

THIRD WITCH.   There to meet with Macbeth.

FIRST WITCH.   I come, Graymalkin.   8

SECOND WITCH.   Paddock calls.   9

THIRD WITCH.   Anon. Fair is foul, and foul is fair.

ALL.   Hover through the fog and filthy air.

                                                            Exeunt.   11

SCENE 2

King Duncan and others hear from a wounded sergeant that Macbeth has killed the traitor Macdonwald. Ross arrives to report that Macbeth's forces were victorious, the Thane of Cawdor was defeated, and the King of Norway was forced to pay before being allowed to bury his dead. Duncan sentences the Thane of Cawdor to death and requests that Macbeth be told that he is the new Thane of Cawdor.

s.d.   **Forres**   a town in northern Scotland.

s.d.   **Alarum**   noise of battle offstage.

6   **broil**   battle.

13   **kerns . . . gallowglasses**   Irish soldiers, the latter armed with axes.

14–20   **Fortune . . . slave**   Fortune, like a harlot who smiles on anyone, first favored Macdonwald, but then Macbeth fought with his sword (steel) until he faced Macdonwald (the slave).

22   **unseamed . . . nave . . . chops**   slashed him from the navel to the jaws.

A *camp near Forres.*

n

Alarum within. Enter DUNCAN, MALCOLM, DONALBAIN,
LENNOX, *with* ATTENDANTS, *meeting a bleeding*
SERGEANT.

n

DUNCAN.   What bloody man is that? He can report,
As seemeth by his plight, of the revolt
The newest state.

MALCOLM.   This is the sergeant
Who like a good and hardy soldier fought
'Gainst my captivity. Hail, brave friend!
Say to the king the knowledge of the broil
As thou didst leave it.

6

SERGEANT.   Doubtful it stood,
As two spent swimmers that do cling together
And choke their art. The merciless Macdonwald—
Worthy to be a rebel, for to that
The multiplying villainies of nature
Do swarm upon him—from the Western Isles
Of kerns and gallowglasses is supplied;
And Fortune, on his damnèd quarrel smiling,
Showed like a rebel's whore. But all's too weak;
For brave Macbeth—well he deserves that name—
Disdaining Fortune, with his brandished steel,
Which smoked with bloody execution,
Like valor's minion carved out his passage
Till he faced the slave;
Which ne'er shook hands nor bade farewell to him
Till he unseamed him from the nave to th' chops,
And fixed his head upon our battlements.

13

14

22

DUNCAN.   O valiant cousin! worthy gentleman!

SERGEANT.   As whence the sun 'gins his reflection
Shipwrecking storms and direful thunders break,
So from that spring whence comfort seemed to come
Discomfort swells. Mark, King of Scotland, mark.

31   **Norweyan**   Norwegian.

40   **memorize . . . Golgotha**   make the scene as memorable as
        Golgotha, the place where Jesus was crucified. *Golgotha*
        means "place of a skull."

45   **Thane**   a noble, a Scottish title.

48   **Fife**   a county in eastern Scotland.

50   **Norway himself**   the Norwegian king.

No sooner justice had, with valor armed,
Compelled these skipping kerns to trust their heels,
But the Norweyan lord, surveying vantage,   31
With furbished arms and new supplies of men,
Began a fresh assault.

DUNCAN.   Dismayed not this
Our captains, Macbeth and Banquo?

SERGEANT.   Yes,
As sparrows eagles, or the hare the lion.
If I say sooth, I must report they were
As cannons overcharged with double cracks, so they
Doubly redoubled strokes upon the foe.
Except they meant to bathe in reeking wounds,
Or memorize another Golgotha,   40
I cannot tell—
But I am faint; my gashes cry for help.

DUNCAN.   So well thy words become thee as thy
    wounds;
They smack of honor both. Go get him surgeons.
                              Exit SERGEANT, *attended.*
Who comes here?

                    Enter ROSS *and* ANGUS.

MALCOLM.   The worthy Thane of Ross.   45

LENNOX.   What a haste looks through his eyes! So
    should he look
That seems to speak things strange.

ROSS.   God save the King!

DUNCAN.   Whence camest thou, worthy thane?

ROSS.   From Fife, great King,   48
Where the Norweyan banners flout the sky
And fan our people cold. Norway himself,   50
With terrible numbers,
Assisted by that most disloyal traitor
The Thane of Cawdor, began a dismal conflict,

54 **Bellona's bridegroom, lapped in proof** Macbeth dressed in armor. Bellona was the Roman goddess of war.

59 **composition** a truce or peace treaty.

61 **Saint Colme's inch** Inchcolm, the isle of St. Columba. *Inch* is Scots for "island."

Till that Bellona's bridegroom, lapped in proof,   54
Confronted him with self-comparisons,
Point against point, rebellious arm 'gainst arm,
Curbing his lavish spirit: and to conclude,
The victory fell on us.

DUNCAN.   Great happiness!

ROSS.   That now
Sweno, the Norways' king, craves composition;   59
Nor would we deign him burial of his men
Till he disbursèd at Saint Colme's inch   61
Ten thousand dollars to our general use.

DUNCAN.   No more that Thane of Cawdor shall deceive
Our bosom interest. Go pronounce his present death,
And with his former title greet Macbeth.

ROSS.   I'll see it done.

DUNCAN.   What he hath lost, noble Macbeth hath won.
                                      Exeunt.

SCENE 3

The witches reveal the supernatural nature of their activities, greet Macbeth as Thane of Glamis and then Thane of Cawdor, and prophesy that he will be king. For Banquo they prophesy that not he but his children will be kings. Ross and Angus arrive to inform Macbeth that he is indeed now Thane of Cawdor.

A heath.

Thunder. Enter the three WITCHES.

FIRST WITCH.   Where hast thou been, sister?

SECOND WITCH.   Killing swine.

THIRD WITCH.   Sister, where thou?

5   **mounched**   munched, chewed with the mouth closed.

6   **aroint thee**   go away; **rump-fed ronyon** mangy creature who eats refuse.

7   **Aleppo**   city in Syria; *Tiger*   the sailor's ship.

8–9   **But . . . tail**   Witches were thought to be able to use sieves as boats and to take the shape of an animal, but usually with a defect, such as a tailless rat.

17   **shipman's card**   card showing the points of the compass.

20   **penthouse lid**   eyelid.

22   **sev'nnights**   weeks.

24   **bark**   small ship

32   **Weird Sisters**   the witches. *Weird*, originally a noun, is an old word meaning "fate."

33   **Posters**   swift travelers.

FIRST WITCH.   A sailor's wife had chestnuts in her lap,
  And mounched, and mounched, and mounched.
    "Give me," quoth I.   5
  "Aroint thee, witch!" the rump-fed ronyon cries.   6
  Her husband's to Aleppo gone, master o' the *Tiger*;   7
  But in a sieve I'll thither sail,   8
  And, like a rat without a tail,
  I'll do, I'll do, and I'll do.

SECOND WITCH.   I'll give thee a wind.

FIRST WITCH.   Thou'rt kind.

THIRD WITCH.   And I another.

FIRST WITCH.   I myself have all the other,
  And the very ports they blow,
  All the quarters that they know
  I' th' shipman's card.   17
  I will drain him dry as hay.
  Sleep shall neither night nor day
  Hang upon his penthouse lid.   20
  He shall live a man forbid.
  Weary sev'nnights nine times nine   22
  Shall he dwindle, peak, and pine.
  Though his bark cannot be lost,   24
  Yet it shall be tempest-tossed.
  Look what I have.

SECOND WITCH.   Show me, show me.

FIRST WITCH.   Here I have a pilot's thumb,
  Wrecked as homeward he did come.

                                          Drum within.

THIRD WITCH.   A drum, a drum!
  Macbeth doth come.

ALL.   The Weird Sisters, hand in hand,   32
  Posters of the sea and land,   33
  Thus do go about, about,
  Thrice to thine, and thrice to mine,
  And thrice again, to make up nine.
  Peace! The charm's wound up.

55   **grace** honor.

66   **happy** fortunate.

Enter MACBETH *and* BANQUO.

MACBETH.   So foul and fair a day I have not seen.

BANQUO.   How far is't called to Forres? — What are
    these,
So withered and so wild in their attire,
That look not like th' inhabitants o' the earth,
And yet are on't? Live you? Or are you aught
That man may question? You seem to understand me,
By each at once her chappy finger laying
Upon her skinny lips. You should be women,
And yet your beards forbid me to interpret
That you are so.

MACBETH.   Speak, if you can. What are you?

FIRST WITCH.   All hail, Macbeth! Hail to thee, Thane
    of Glamis!

SECOND WITCH.   All hail, Macbeth! Hail to thee,
    Thane of Cawdor!

THIRD WITCH.   All hail, Macbeth, that shalt be king
    hereafter!

BANQUO.   Good sir, why do you start and seem to fear
Things that do sound so fair? I' th' name of truth,
Are ye fantastical, or that indeed
Which outwardly ye show? My noble partner
You greet with present grace and great prediction   55
Of noble having and of royal hope,
That he seems rapt withal. To me you speak not.
If you can look into the seeds of time
And say which grain will grow and which will not,
Speak then to me, who neither beg nor fear
Your favors nor your hate.

FIRST WITCH.   Hail!

SECOND WITCH.   Hail!

THIRD WITCH.   Hail!

FIRST WITCH.   Lesser than Macbeth, and greater.

SECOND WITCH.   Not so happy, yet much happier.   66

67   **get**   beget.

71   **Sinel's death**   Sinel was the former Thane of Glamis and Macbeth's father.

81   **corporal**   belonging to the material world; bodily.

84   **insane root**   root that makes one insane; hemlock.

THIRD WITCH.   Thou shalt get kings, though thou be
   none.   67
  So all hail, Macbeth and Banquo!

FIRST WITCH.   Banquo and Macbeth, all hail!

MACBETH.   Stay, you imperfect speakers, tell me more!
  By Sinel's death I know I am Thane of Glamis,   71
  But how of Cawdor? The Thane of Cawdor lives,
  A prosperous gentleman; and to be king
  Stands not within the prospect of belief,
  No more than to be Cawdor. Say from whence
  You owe this strange intelligence, or why
  Upon this blasted heath you stop our way
  With such prophetic greeting? Speak, I charge you.
                                       WITCHES *vanish*.

BANQUO.   The earth hath bubbles, as the water has,
  And these are of them. Whither are they vanished?

MACBETH.   Into the air, and what seemed corporal
  melted   81
  As breath into the wind. Would they had stayed!

BANQUO.   Were such things here as we do speak about?
  Or have we eaten on the insane root   84
  That takes the reason prisoner?

MACBETH.   Your children shall be kings.

BANQUO.   You shall be king.

MACBETH.   And Thane of Cawdor too. Went it not so?

BANQUO.   To th' selfsame tune and words. Who's here?

Enter ROSS *and* ANGUS.

ROSS.   The king hath happily received, Macbeth,
  The news of thy success; and when he reads
  Thy personal venture in the rebels' fight,
  His wonders and his praises do contend
  Which should be thine or his. Silenced with that,
  In viewing o'er the rest o' th' selfsame day,
  He finds thee in the stout Norweyan ranks,
  Nothing afeard of what thyself didst make,

104   **earnest** a promise.

112   **line** support.

115   **treasons capital** capital treasons; that is, the crime of treason punishable by death.

120   **trusted home** believed totally.

Strange images of death. As thick as hail
Came post with post, and every one did bear
Thy praises in his kingdom's great defense,
And poured them down before him.

ANGUS.   We are sent
To give thee from our royal master thanks;
Only to herald thee into his sight,
Not pay thee.

ROSS.   And for an earnest of a greater honor,   104
He bade me, from him, call thee Thane of Cawdor;
In which addition, hail, most worthy thane!
For it is thine.

BANQUO.   What, can the devil speak true?

MACBETH.   The Thane of Cawdor lives. Why do you
    dress me
In borrowed robes?

ANGUS.   Who was the thane lives yet,
But under heavy judgment bears that life
Which he deserve to lose. Whether he was combined
With those of Norway, or did line the rebel   112
With hidden help and vantage, or that with both
He labored in his country's wrack, I know not;
But treasons capital, confessed and proved,   115
Have overthrown him.

MACBETH.   (aside)   Glamis, and Thane of Cawdor!
The greatest is behind. (to ROSS and ANGUS) Thanks
    for your pains.
(aside to BANQUO) Do you not hope your children
    shall be kings,
When those that gave the Thane of Cawdor to me
Promised no less to them?

BANQUO.   (aside to MACBETH)   That, trusted home,   120
Might yet enkindle you unto the crown,
Besides the Thane of Cawdor. But 'tis strange;
And oftentimes, to win us to our harm,
The instruments of darkness tell us truths,

19

135   **unfix my hair**   make my hair stand on end.

145–146 **strange garments, cleave not . . . use**   a metaphorical expression; Banquo thinks Macbeth's new honors are like new clothes that take getting used to.

Win us with honest trifles, to betray 's
In deepest consequence.—
(*to* ROSS *and* ANGUS) Cousins, a word, I pray you.

MACBETH.   (*aside*)   Two truths are told,
As happy prologues to the swelling act
Of the imperial theme.—I thank you, gentlemen.
(*aside*) This supernatural soliciting
Cannot be ill; cannot be good. If ill,
Why hath it given me earnest of success,
Commencing in a truth? I am Thane of Cawdor.
If good, why do I yield to that suggestion
Whose horrid image doth unfix my hair   135
And make my seated heart knock at my ribs,
Against the use of nature? Present fears
Are less than horrible imaginings.
My thought, whose murder yet is but fantastical,
Shakes so my single state of man that function
Is smothered in surmise, and nothing is
But what is not.

BANQUO.   Look, how our partner's rapt.

MACBETH.   (*aside*) If chance will have me king, why,
    chance may crown me
Without my stir.

BANQUO.   New honors come upon him,
Like our strange garments, cleave not to their mold   145
But with the aid of use.

MACBETH.   (*aside*)   Come what come may,
Time and the hour runs through the roughest day.

BANQUO.   Worthy Macbeth, we stay upon your leisure.

MACBETH.   Give me your favor. My dull brain was
    wrought
With things forgotten. Kind gentlemen, your pains
Are registered where every day I turn
The leaf to read them. Let us toward the King.

s.d.   **Flourish**   trumpet fanfare to announce the king.

2   **liege**   (lēj) lord.

(*aside to* BANQUO) Think upon what hath chanced,
    and at more time,
The interim having weighed it, let us speak
Our free hearts each to other.

BANQUO.   Very gladly.

MACBETH.   Till then, enough. — Come, friends.

                                   Exeunt.

SCENE 4

Malcolm informs King Duncan that the former Thane of Cawdor has been executed. The King states that he will name Malcolm the Prince of Cumberland and thus successor to the throne. When he then expresses his desire to travel to Inverness and Macbeth's castle, Macbeth says he wishes to leave to tell his wife of the King's impending arrival.

Forres. The palace.

Flourish. Enter DUNCAN, MALCOLM, DONALBAIN,   n
           LENNOX, *and* ATTENDANTS.

DUNCAN.   Is execution done on Cawdor? Are not
    Those in commission yet returned?

MALCOLM.   My liege,   2
    They are not yet come back. But I have spoke
    With one that saw him die, who did report
    That very frankly he confessed his treasons,
    Implored your Highness' pardon and set forth
    A deep repentance. Nothing in his life
    Became him like the leaving it. He died
    As one that had been studied in his death
    To throw away the dearest thing he owed
    As 'twere a careless trifle.

16   **before**   ahead (in deserving).

39   **Prince of Cumberland**   title of the one who would succeed
        to the Scottish throne.

DUNCAN. There's no art
To find the mind's construction in the face.
He was a gentleman on whom I built
An absolute trust.

Enter MACBETH, BANQUO, ROSS, *and* ANGUS.
O worthiest cousin!
The sin of my ingratitude even now
Was heavy on me. Thou art so far before   16
That swiftest wing of recompense is slow
To overtake thee. Would thou hadst less deserved,
That the proportion both of thanks and payment
Might have been mine! Only I have left to say,
More is thy due than more than all can pay.

MACBETH.   The service and the loyalty I owe,
In doing it, pays itself. Your Highness' part
Is to receive our duties; and our duties
Are to your throne and state children and servants,
Which do but what they should, by doing every thing
Safe toward your love and honor.

DUNCAN.   Welcome hither.
I have begun to plant thee, and will labor
To make thee full of growing. Noble Banquo,
That hast no less deserved, nor must be known
No less to have done so, let me infold thee
And hold thee to my heart.

BANQUO.   There if I grow,
The harvest is your own.

DUNCAN.   My plenteous joys,
Wanton in fullness, seek to hide themselves
In drops of sorrow. Sons, kinsmen, thanes,
And you whose places are the nearest, know,
We will establish our estate upon
Our eldest, Malcolm, whom we name hereafter
The Prince of Cumberland; which honor must   39
Not unaccompanied invest him only,

42   **Inverness**   (in'vėr nes') the site of Macbeth's castle, Dunsinane, in northern Scotland.

45   **harbinger**   (har'bin jėr) messenger.

But signs of nobleness, like stars, shall shine
On all deservers. From hence to Inverness,   42
And bind us further to you.

MACBETH.   The rest is labor, which is not used for you.
I'll be myself the harbinger, and make joyful   45
The hearing of my wife with your approach;
So humbly take my leave.

DUNCAN.   My worthy Cawdor!

MACBETH.   (*aside*) The prince of Cumberland! That is a
     step
On which I must fall down, or else o'erleap,
For in my way it lies. Stars, hide your fires;
Let not light see my black and deep desires.
The eye wink at the hand; yet let that be
Which the eye fears, when it is done, to see.

Exit.

DUNCAN.   True, worthy Banquo; he is full so valiant,
And in his commendations I am fed;
It is a banquet to me. Let's after him,
Whose care is gone before to bid us welcome.
It is a peerless kinsman.

Flourish. Exeunt.

SCENE 5

*After Lady Macbeth reads aloud from Macbeth's letter, she expresses fear that
Macbeth will not have the courage to seize the throne. When she is informed that the
King is about to arrive, she realizes that this is an opportunity to kill Duncan and
assure that her husband will be king. When Macbeth arrives, she tells him
to mask his worries by showing a welcome face and says that she will take charge
of "this night's great business."*

28   **golden round**   the crown.

29   **metaphysical**   supernatural.

Inverness. Macbeth's castle.

Enter LADY MACBETH *alone, with a letter.*

LADY MACBETH.   "They met me in the day of success;
and I have learned by the perfect'st report, they
have more in them than mortal knowledge. When I
burned in desire to question them further, they
made themselves air, into which they vanished.
Whiles I stood rapt in the wonder of it, came
missives from the king, who all-hailed me 'Thane of
Cawdor,' by which title, before, these Weird Sisters
saluted me, and referred me to the coming on of
time, with 'Hail, king that shalt be!' This have I
thought good to deliver thee, my dearest partner of
greatness, that thou mightst not lose the dues of
rejoicing by being ignorant of what greatness is
promised thee. Lay it to thy heart, and farewell."
Glamis thou art, and Cawdor, and shalt be
What thou art promised. Yet do I fear thy nature;
It is too full o' the milk of human kindness
To catch the nearest way. Thou wouldst be great,
Art not without ambition, but without
The illness should attend it. What thou wouldst
   highly,
That wouldst thou holily; wouldst not play false,
And yet wouldst wrongly win. Thou 'ldst have, great
   Glamis,
That which cries "Thus thou must do," if thou have
   it;
And that which rather thou dost fear to do
Than wishest should be undone. Hie thee hither,
That I may pour my spirits in thine ear
And chastise with the valor of my tongue
All that impedes thee from the golden round   28
Which fate and metaphysical aid doth seem   29
To have thee crowned withal.

41   **mortal thoughts**   thoughts of death, murderous thoughts; **unsex me**   deprive me of my feminine, or softer, nature.

45   **compunctious . . . nature**   natural feelings of pity.

48   **murdering ministers**   evil angels or agents.

49   **sightless**   invisible.

51   **pall**   (pôl) wrap; **dunnest**   darkest.

Enter MESSENGER.
                         What is your tidings?

MESSENGER.   The king comes here tonight.

LADY MACBETH.   Thou 'rt mad to say it!
   Is not thy master with him, who, were 't so,
   Would have informed for preparation?

MESSENGER.   So please you, it is true. Our thane is
      coming.
   One of my fellows had the speed of him,
   Who, almost dead for breath, had scarcely more
   Than would make up his message.

LADY MACBETH.   Give him tending;
   He brings great news.
                              Exit MESSENGER.
                    The raven himself is hoarse
   That croaks the fatal entrance of Duncan
   Under my battlements. Come, you spirits
   That tend on mortal thoughts, unsex me here,   41
   And fill me, from the crown to the toe, top-full
   Of direst cruelty! Make thick my blood;
   Stop up th' access and passage to remorse,
   That no compunctious visitings of nature   45
   Shake my fell purpose, nor keep peace between
   Th' effect and it! Come to my woman's breasts,
   And take my milk for gall, you murdering ministers,   48
   Wherever in your sightless substances   49
   You wait on nature's mischief! Come, thick night,
   And pall thee in the dunnest smoke of hell,   51
   That my keen knife see not the wound it makes,
   Nor heaven peep through the blanket of the dark,
   To cry "Hold, hold!"

            Enter MACBETH.
            Great Glamis! Worthy Cawdor!
   Greater than both, by the all-hail hereafter!

31

71   **look up clear**   appear untroubled.

72   **to . . . fear**   to look troubled is to arouse suspicion.

Thy letters have transported me beyond
This ignorant present, and I feel now
The future in the instant.

MACBETH.   My dearest love,
Duncan comes here tonight.

LADY MACBETH.   And when goes hence?

MACBETH.   Tomorrow, as he purposes.

LADY MACBETH.   O, never
Shall sun that morrow see!
Your face, my thane, is as a book where men
May read strange matters. To beguile the time,
Look like the time; bear welcome in your eye,
Your hand, your tongue. Look like th' innocent
    flower,
But be the serpent under 't. He that's coming
Must be provided for; and you shall put
This night's great business into my dispatch,
Which shall to all our nights and days to come
Give solely sovereign sway and masterdom.

MACBETH.   We will speak further.

LADY MACBETH.   Only look up clear.   71
To alter favor ever is to fear.   72
Leave all the rest to me.

                                        Exeunt.

SCENE 6

When Duncan and the other guests arrive, the King expresses delight in the castle surroundings; Banquo agrees that it is a pleasant place. All are greeted warmly by Lady Macbeth, and Duncan expresses his love for Macbeth.

33

s.d.   **hautboys**   (hō'bois) oboes, high-pitched wind instruments.

1   **seat**   site.

4   **martlet**   martin, a bird of the swallow family.

6–7   **jutty . . . coign of vantage**   all terms referring to parts of a building where the bird nests.

11–14   **The love . . . trouble**   Duncan means that even though he has caused them trouble by his visit, they should thank him because his presence means that he loves them.

20   **We rest your hermits**   We remain as those who will pray for you as hermits do. Originally a hermit was one who lived a reclusive life for religious reasons.

21   **course**   chased.

22   **purveyor**   forerunner.

Before Macbeth's castle.

Hautboys and torches. Enter DUNCAN, MALCOLM,
DONALBAIN, BANQUO, LENNOX, MACDUFF,
ROSS, ANGUS, *and* ATTENDANTS.

DUNCAN.   This castle hath a pleasant seat. The air   1
Nimbly and sweetly recommends itself
Unto our gentle senses.

BANQUO.   This guest of summer,
The temple-haunting martlet, does approve   4
By his loved mansionry that the heaven's breath
Smells wooingly here. No jutty, frieze,   6
Buttress, nor coign of vantage, but this bird
Hath made his pendent bed and procreant cradle.
Where they most breed and haunt, I have observed
The air is delicate.

Enter LADY MACBETH.

DUNCAN.   See, see, our honored hostess!
The love that follows us sometime is our trouble,   11
Which still we thank as love. Herein I teach you
How you shall bid God 'ild us for your pains,
And thank us for your trouble.

LADY MACBETH.   All our service
In every point twice done, and then done double,
Were poor and single business to contend
Against those honors deep and broad wherewith
Your Majesty loads our house. For those of old,
And the late dignities heaped up to them,
We rest your hermits.

DUNCAN.   Where's the Thane of Cawdor?   20
We coursed him at the heels, and had a purpose   21
To be his purveyor; but he rides well,   22
And his great love, sharp as his spur, hath holp him
To his home before us. Fair and noble hostess,
We are your guest tonight.

25–28   **Your servants . . . own**   As your servants, what we have is yours, and we will make an account of it when you wish.

s.d.   **Sewer . . . divers Servants**   chief server and various other servants.

3   **trammel up**   entangle in a net.

4   **surcease**   stoppage; that is, Duncan's death. In lines 2–4, Macbeth wishes that the murder could have no future consequences.

7   **jump**   risk.

LADY MACBETH.   Your servants ever   25
  Have theirs, themselves, and what is theirs, in compt
  To make their audit at your Highness' pleasure,
  Still to return your own.

DUNCAN.   Give me your hand;
  Conduct me to mine host. We love him highly
  And shall continue our graces towards him.
  By your leave, hostess.

                                        Exeunt.

SCENE 7

Macbeth contemplates the assassination of the King and tells Lady Macbeth that he cannot continue with their plans. She upbraids him and reveals that she will make Duncan's two attendants drunk so that the King will sleep unguarded. Macbeth finally agrees to go ahead with the murder.

Macbeth's castle.

Hautboys and torches. Enter a SEWER, *and divers*   n
SERVANTS *with dishes and service, and pass
over the stage. Then enter* MACBETH.

MACBETH.   If it were done when 'tis done, then 'twere
    well
  It were done quickly. If th' assassination
  Could trammel up the consequence, and catch,   3
  With his surcease, success; that but this blow   4
  Might be the be-all and the end-all here,
  But here, upon this bank and shoal of time,
  We 'ld jump the life to come. But in these cases   7
  We still have judgment here, that we but teach
  Bloody instructions, which, being taught, return
  To plague th' inventor. This even-handed justice

20   **taking-off**   murder.

22   **cherubin**   members of the second order of angels.

25–28   **I . . . other**   Ambition is first compared to a spur that urges him on. Then, ambition is like a rider who jumps into his saddle but falls off the other side of the horse.

39–41   **Art thou afeard . . . desire?**   Are you afraid to be as brave in your actions as you are in your desire?

Commends th' ingredience of our poisoned chalice
To our own lips. He's here in double trust:
First, as I am his kinsman and his subject,
Strong both against the deed; then, as the host,
Who should against his murderer shut the door,
Not bear the knife myself. Besides, this Duncan
Hath borne his faculties so meek, hath been
So clear in his great office, that his virtues
Will plead like angels, trumpet-tongued, against
The deep damnation of his taking-off;   20
And pity, like a naked new-born babe,
Striding the blast, or heaven's cherubin, horsed   22
Upon the sightless couriers of the air,
Shall blow the horrid deed in every eye,
That tears shall drown the wind. I have no spur   25
To prick the sides of my intent, but only
Vaulting ambition, which o'erleaps itself
And falls on the other —

reasons
not to
kill

       Enter LADY MACBETH.
              How now! What news?

LADY MACBETH.   He has almost supped. Why have you
   left the chamber?

MACBETH.   Hath he asked for me?

LADY MACBETH.   ·   Know you not he has?

MACBETH.   We will proceed no further in this business.
   He hath honored me of late, and I have bought
   Golden opinions from all sorts of people,
   Which would be worn now in their newest gloss,
   Not cast aside so soon.

LADY MACBETH.   Was the hope drunk
   Wherein you dressed yourself? Hath it slept since?
   And wakes it now, to look so green and pale
   At what it did so freely? From this time
   Such I account thy love. Art thou afeard   39
   To be the same in thine own act and valor
   As thou art in desire? Wouldst thou have that

45   **cat . . . adage**   "The cat would eat fish, but would not wet her feet"; **Prithee**   pray thee, please.

47–49   **What beast . . . man**   You were a man when you dared to do the deed; that is, if you were not a man when you suggested the murder, what kind of beast were you?

52   **adhere**   agree.

60   **screw . . . sticking place**   The allusion is to a crossbow, a medieval weapon. The bowman pulled the bowstring toward himself by a crank, and the string was then held in a notch (sticking place) until the arrow was released.

63   **chamberlains**   (chām'ber lins) attendants in a bedchamber.

64   **wassail**   (was' l *or* was āl') drink, revelry.

65–67   **memory . . . only**   Memory and reason will succumb to the fumes of wine and be as a distillery. An *alembic* (limbeck) is an apparatus used for distilling.

Which thou esteem'st the ornament of life,
And live a coward in thine own esteem,
Letting "I dare not" wait upon "I would,"
Like the poor cat i' th' adage?

MACBETH.   Prithee, peace!   45
I dare do all that may become a man;
Who dares do more is none.

LADY MACBETH.   What beast was't then   47
That made you break this enterprise to me?
When you durst do it, then you were a man;
And, to be more than what you were, you would
Be so much more the man. Nor time nor place
Did then adhere, and yet you would make both.   52
They have made themselves, and that their fitness
   now
Does unmake you. I have given suck, and know
How tender 'tis to love the babe that milks me;
I would, while it was smiling in my face,
Have plucked my nipple from his boneless gums
And dashed the brains out, had I so sworn as you
Have done to this.

MACBETH.   If we should fail?

LADY MACBETH.   We fail?
But screw your courage to the sticking place   60
And we'll not fail. When Duncan is asleep—
Whereto the rather shall his day's hard journey
Soundly invite him—his two chamberlains   63
Will I with wine and wassail so convince,   64
That memory, the warder of the brain,   65
Shall be a fume, and the receipt of reason
A limbeck only. When in swinish sleep
Their drenchèd natures lie as in a death,
What cannot you and I perform upon
Th' unguarded Duncan? What not put upon
His spongy officers, who shall bear the guilt
Of our great quell?

72   **quell**   murder.

73   **undaunted mettle**   unafraid, or brave, spirit.

79–80   **I . . . feat**   He directs all his energies to the deed. *Bend up* means "to stretch tight," as one would an archer's bow.

[handwritten annotation: she's only capable of bearing ruthless male kids instead soft Females]

MACBETH.   Bring forth men-children only;   72
For thy undaunted mettle should compose   73
Nothing but males. Will it not be received,
When we have marked with blood those sleepy two
Of his own chamber and used their very daggers,
That they have done't?

LADY MACBETH.   Who dares receive it other,
As we shall make our griefs and clamor roar
Upon his death?

MACBETH.   I am settled, and bend up   79
Each corporal agent to this terrible feat.
Away, and mock the time with fairest show.
False face must hide what the false heart doth know.

                                        Exeunt.

MACBETH

ACT II

"I have done the deed. Didst thou not hear a noise?"

4   **husbandry** economy.

5   **Take thee that too** Banquo probably gives Fleance his dagger as well as his sword.

14   **Sent . . . largess . . . offices** sent gifts to the servants' quarters.

15   **withal** with.

16–17   **shut up . . . content** ended his day contented.

SCENE 1

Banquo, unable to sleep, tells Macbeth that he dreamed of the Weird Sisters. Macbeth replies that he wants to discuss "that business" when Banquo has time and asks for Banquo's support when the witches' prophecies are fulfilled. When Banquo leaves, Macbeth thinks he sees a dagger but cannot decide whether it is real or not. At Lady Macbeth's signal, he goes forward to kill Duncan.

Inverness. Court of Macbeth's castle.

Enter BANQUO, *and* FLEANCE, *with a torch before him.*

BANQUO.   How goes the night, boy?

FLEANCE.   The moon is down; I have not heard the
    clock.

BANQUO.   And she goes down at twelve.

FLEANCE.   I take 't, 'tis later, sir.

BANQUO.   Hold, take my sword. There's husbandry in
    heaven,   4
Their candles are all out. Take thee that too.   5
A heavy summons lies like lead upon me,
And yet I would not sleep. Merciful powers,
Restrain in me the cursèd thoughts that nature
Gives way to in repose!

Enter MACBETH, *and a* SERVANT *with a torch.*
             Give me my sword.

Who's there?

MACBETH.   A friend.

BANQUO.   What, sir, not yet at rest? The King's abed.
He hath been in unusual pleasure, and
Sent forth great largess to your offices.   14
This diamond he greets your wife withal,   15
By the name of most kind hostess, and shut up   16
In measureless content.

17–19   **Being . . . wrought**   We would have entertained more lavishly, had we been more prepared.

25   **cleave to my consent**   give me your allegiance or support.

27–28   **keep . . . bosom franchised . . . allegiance clear**   Banquo wants to have a clear conscience and retain his loyalty to Duncan.

36–37   **sensible to feeling**   perceptible to the senses.

41   **As this . . . draw**   Macbeth may draw his own dagger here.

MACBETH.   Being unprepared,   17
  Our will became the servant to defect,
  Which else should free have wrought.

BANQUO.   All's well.
  I dreamt last night of the three Weird Sisters.
  To you they have showed some truth.

MACBETH.   I think not of them.
  Yet, when we can entreat an hour to serve,
  We would spend it in some words upon that business,
  If you would grant the time.

BANQUO.   At your kind'st leisure.

MACBETH.   If you shall cleave to my consent when 'tis,   25
  It shall make honor for you.

BANQUO.   So I lose none
  In seeking to augment it, but still keep   27
  My bosom franchised and allegiance clear,
  I shall be counseled.

MACBETH.   Good repose the while!

BANQUO.   Thanks, sir. The like to you!
                          Exeunt BANQUO *with* FLEANCE.

MACBETH.   Go bid thy mistress, when my drink is ready,
  She strike upon the bell. Get thee to bed.
                          Exit SERVANT.

  Is this a dagger which I see before me,
  The handle toward my hand? Come, let me clutch
      thee.
  I have thee not, and yet I see thee still.   *hallucinate*
  Art thou not, fatal vision, sensible   *stress* *fool*   36
  To feeling as to sight? Or art thou but *cuz*
  A dagger of the mind, a false creation,   *guilt*
  Proceeding from the heat-oppressèd brain?
  I see thee yet, in form as palpable
  As this which now I draw.   41
  Thou marshall'st me the way that I was going,
  And such an instrument I was to use.

46   **dudgeon**   hilt of the dagger.

51–56   **Witchcraft . . . ghost**   Hecate (hek'it) was a Greek goddess of the moon and later of witchcraft, to whom believers gave offerings. The wolf howls the time for murder and, in his approach (stealthy pace), is compared to the criminal approach of Tarquin, the son of a Roman king, who raped a married woman named Lucretia.

58–59   **stones prate . . . time**   Even the stones chatter in a tone of horror.

61   **Words . . . gives**   Cool words are not a substitute for action.

Mine eyes are made the fools o' th' other senses,
Or else worth all the rest. I see thee still,
And on thy blade and dudgeon gouts of blood,   46
Which was not so before. There's no such thing.
It is the bloody business which informs
Thus to mine eyes. Now o'er the one half-world
Nature seems dead, and wicked dreams abuse
The curtained sleep. Witchcraft celebrates   51
Pale Hecate's offerings; and withered murder,
Alarumed by his sentinel, the wolf,
Whose howl's his watch, thus with his stealthy pace,
With Tarquin's ravishing strides, towards his design
Moves like a ghost. Thou sure and firm-set earth,
Hear not my steps which way they walk, for fear
Thy very stones prate of my whereabout   58
And take the present horror from the time
Which now suits with it. Whiles I threat, he lives;
Words to the heat of deeds too cold breath gives.   61

A bell rings.

I go, and it is done. The bell invites me.
Hear it not, Duncan, for it is a knell
That summons thee to heaven, or to hell.

Exit.

SCENE 2

Lady Macbeth awaits Macbeth, and he appears to announce that he has "done the deed." When he refuses to return the bloody daggers, which he still carries, Lady Macbeth does so. Both of them hear a knocking at an outer door and quickly retire to their chamber.

The same.

Enter LADY MACBETH.

3   **owl . . . fatal bellman**   An owl's screech was often considered an omen of death. In Shakespeare's time a bellman rang a bell to announce a death, perhaps of one scheduled for execution.

5   **surfeited grooms**   servants who have overindulged in wine.

6   **drugged their possets**   put a drug in their bedtime drink. A *posset* was a hot drink made with milk, wine, and spices.

9   **Alack**   (ə lak') an expression of surprise or dismay.

LADY MACBETH.   That which hath made them drunk
    hath made me bold;
  What hath quenched them hath given me fire. Hark!
    Peace!
  It was the owl that shrieked, the fatal bellman,   3
  Which gives the stern'st good-night. He is about it.
  The doors are open, and the surfeited grooms   5
  Do mock their charge with snores. I have drugged
    their possets,   6
  That death and nature do contend about them,
  Whether they live or die.

MACBETH.   (*within*)   Who's there? What, ho!

LADY MACBETH.   Alack, I am afraid they have awaked,   9
  And 'tis not done. Th' attempt and not the deed
  Confounds us. Hark! I laid their daggers ready;
  He could not miss 'em. Had he not resembled
  My father as he slept, I had done't.

                    Enter MACBETH.
                              My husband!

MACBETH.   I have done the deed. Didst thou not hear
  a noise?

LADY MACBETH.   I heard the owl scream and the
  crickets cry.
  Did not you speak?

MACBETH.   When?

LADY MACBETH.   Now.

MACBETH.   As I descended?

LADY MACBETH.   Ay.

MACBETH.   Hark! Who lies i' the second chamber?

LADY MACBETH.   Donalbain.

MACBETH.   (*looking on his hands*) This is a sorry sight.

LADY MACBETH.   A foolish thought, to say a sorry sight.

29   **two lodged together**   Malcolm and Donalbain.

31   **As they had seen me**   As *if* they had seen me.

35   **But wherefore . . . ?**   But why . . . ?

41   **raveled sleave**   tangled or twisted thread or yarn.

MACBETH.   There's one did laugh in 's sleep, and one
    cried "Murder!"
That they did wake each other. I stood and heard
    them.
But they did say their prayers, and addressed them
Again to sleep.

LADY MACBETH.   There are two lodged together.   29

MACBETH.   One cried "God bless us!" and "Amen!" the
    other,
As they had seen me with these hangman's hands.   31
List'ning their fear, I could not say "Amen"
When they did say "God bless us!"

LADY MACBETH.   Consider it not so deeply.

MACBETH.   But wherefore could not I pronounce
    "Amen"?   35
I had most need of blessing, and "Amen"
Stuck in my throat.

LADY MACBETH.   These deeds must not be thought
After these ways; so, it will make us mad.

MACBETH.   Methought I heard a voice cry "Sleep no
    more!
Macbeth does murder sleep," the innocent sleep,
Sleep that knits up the raveled sleave of care,   41
The death of each day's life, sore labor's bath,
Balm of hurt minds, great nature's second course,
Chief nourisher in life's feast, —

LADY MACBETH.   What do you mean?

MACBETH.   Still it cried "Sleep no more!" to all the
    house:
"Glamis hath murdered sleep, and therefore Cawdor
Shall sleep no more; Macbeth shall sleep no more."

LADY MACBETH.   Who was it that thus cried? Why,
    worthy thane,
You do unbend your noble strength, to think
So brainsickly of things. Go get some water
And wash this filthy witness from your hand.

57–59   **sleeping . . . eye of childhood . . . devil**   The sleeping and the dead only give the impression of live people, and only children fear such illusions.

65–66   **my hand will . . . incarnadine**   Macbeth's bloody hands will redden the seas.

72–73   **Your constancy . . . unattended**   Your firmness has deserted you.

74   **nightgown**   dressing gown or robe.

Why did you bring these daggers from the place?
They must lie there. Go carry them and smear
The sleepy grooms with blood.

MACBETH.   I'll go no more.
I am afraid to think what I have done;
Look on 't again I dare not.

LADY MACBETH.   Infirm of purpose!
Give me the daggers. The sleeping and the dead   57
Are but as pictures. 'Tis the eye of childhood
That fears a painted devil. If he do bleed,
I'll gild the faces of the grooms withal,
For it must seem their guilt.

                                        Exit. Knock within.
MACBETH.   Whence is that knocking?
How is 't with me, when every noise appalls me?
What hands are here? Ha! They pluck out mine eyes!
Will all great Neptune's ocean wash this blood
Clean from my hand? No, this my hand will rather
The multitudinous seas incarnadine,   65
Making the green one red.

                            Enter LADY MACBETH.
LADY MACBETH.   My hands are of your color, but I
      shame
To wear a heart so white. (*Knock.*) I hear a knocking
At the south entry. Retire we to our chamber.
A little water clears us of this deed.
How easy is it then! Your constancy   72
Hath left you unattended. (*Knock.*) Hark! more
      knocking.
Get on your nightgown, lest occasion call us   74
And show us to be watchers. Be not lost
So poorly in your thoughts.

2   **old**   plenty of

4   **Beelzebub**   (bi el'zi bub) the devil.

5–6   **farmer . . . expectation of plenty**   a farmer who received low prices for his crops instead of the high prices he tried to get, perhaps illegally.

6   **have napkins enow**   have enough handkerchiefs to wipe the sweat caused by hell's heat.

9   **equivocator**   one who speaks ambiguously, often with the intention of misleading. This allusion is thought to refer to the trial in 1606 of Henry Garnet, who was accused of treason.

MACBETH.   To know my deed, 'twere best not know
    myself.

(Knock.)

Wake Duncan with thy knocking! I would thou
    couldst!

Exeunt.

SCENE 3

> As the knocking continues, the Porter tries to make his way to the door while speculating that he is the doorkeeper of hell. Macduff and Lennox enter, and the Porter delivers a speech on the three things that drink causes.
> Macbeth appears and takes Macduff and Lennox to the King's door. Lennox reports on the night's strange happenings as Macduff enters the King's chamber. Macduff reappears, horrified at his discovery. Macbeth kills the guards and defends the act by saying that his love for Duncan overcame reason. Lady Macbeth faints, and Malcolm and Donalbain agree to flee.

The same.

Enter a PORTER. *Knocking within.*

PORTER.   Here's a knocking indeed! If a man were
    porter of hell gate, he should have old   2
    turning the key. (*Knock.*) Knock, knock, knock!
    Who's there, i' the name of Beelzebub? Here's a   4
    farmer that hanged himself on th' expectation of   5
    plenty. Come in time! Have napkins enow about   6
    you; here you'll sweat for 't. (*Knock.*) Knock,
    knock! Who's there, in th' other devil's name?
    Faith, here's an equivocator, that could swear in   9
    both the scales against either scale, who committed
    treason enough for God's sake, yet could not
    equivocate to heaven. O, come in, equivocator.
    (*Knock.*) Knock, knock, knock! Who's there?

59

15   **stealing . . . French hose.** French hose were tight breeches. Either the tailor charged for more cloth than was needed to make the breeches, or he made them as small as he could, thus saving some cloth.

16   **roast your goose** a pun. A *goose* was a tailor's iron, so-called because the shape of the handle resembled a goose's neck.

22   **remember the porter** Here he probably holds out his hand for a tip.

25–26   **second cock** second crow of the rooster; that is, 3 A.M.

28   **Marry . . . nose painting** *Marry* is an oath, "by the Virgin Mary"; drink paints the nose, or makes it red.

Faith, here's an English tailor come hither for
stealing out of a French hose. Come in, tailor. Here   15
you may roast your goose. (*Knock.*) Knock, knock;   16
never at quiet! What are you? But this place is too
cold for hell. I'll devil-porter it no further. I had
thought to have let in some of all professions that
go the primrose way to the everlasting bonfire.
(*Knock.*) Anon, anon! (*Opens the gate.*) I pray you,
remember the porter.   22

Enter MACDUFF *and* LENNOX.

MACDUFF.   Was it so late, friend, ere you went to bed,
That you do lie so late?

PORTER.   Faith, sir, we were carousing till the second
cock; and drink, sir, is a great provoker of three   25
things.

MACDUFF.   What three things does drink especially
provoke?

PORTER.   Marry, sir, nose-painting, sleep, and urine.   28
Lechery, sir, it provokes and unprovokes: it
provokes the desire, but it takes away the
performance. Therefore much drink may be said to
be an equivocator with lechery: it makes him and it
mars him; it sets him on and it takes him off; it
persuades him and disheartens him; makes him
stand to and not stand to; in conclusion,
equivocates him in a sleep and, giving him the lie,
leaves him.

MACDUFF.   I believe drink gave thee the lie last night.

PORTER.   That it did, sir, i' the very throat on me. But I
requited him for his lie, and, I think, being too
strong for him, though he took up my legs
sometimes, yet I made a shift to cast him.

MACDUFF.   Is thy master stirring?

51   **physics pain** cures the pain (of the trouble).

60   **obscure bird** owl, the bird of darkness.

Enter MACBETH.

Our knocking has awaked him; here he comes.

LENNOX.   Good morrow, noble sir.

Exit PORTER.

MACBETH.   Good morrow, both.

MACDUFF.   Is the King stirring, worthy thane?

MACBETH.   Not yet.

MACDUFF.   He did command me to call timely on him;
  I have almost slipped the hour.

MACBETH.   I'll bring you to him.

MACDUFF.   I know this is a joyful trouble to you,
  But yet 'tis one.

MACBETH.   The labor we delight in physics pain.   51
  This is the door.

MACDUFF.   I'll make so bold to call,
  For 'tis my limited service.

Exit MACDUFF.

LENNOX.   Goes the King hence today?

MACBETH.   He does; he did appoint so.

LENNOX.   The night has been unruly. Where we lay,
  Our chimneys were blown down, and, as they say,
  Lamentings heard i' th' air, strange screams of death,
  And prophesying with accents terrible
  Of dire combustion and confused events
  New hatched to the woeful time. The obscure bird   60
  Clamored the livelong night. Some say the earth
  Was feverous and did shake.

MACBETH.   'Twas a rough night.

LENNOX.   My young remembrance cannot parallel
  A fellow to it.

67   **Confusion**   destruction.

69   **The Lord's anointed temple**   allusion to the king as God's representative. In the metaphor the temple is the king's body from whom life has been stolen.

73   **Gorgon**   In Greek mythology, a gorgon was a monster whose appearance could turn one to stone.

79   **great doom's image**   a sight as horrible as that of Judgment Day or the end of the world.

80   **As from your graves . . . sprites**   walk like ghosts from your graves.

81   **countenance**   look upon.

83   **trumpet**   the bell and the shouts. Lady Macbeth's entire speech here and Macduff's speech beginning with line 74 contain a comparison of the present events to the final day of judgment when, at the last trumpet, sleepers (the dead) will awake.

Enter MACDUFF.

MACDUFF.   O horror, horror, horror! Tongue nor heart
   Cannot conceive nor name thee.

MACBETH. ⎫
                                              What's the matter?
LENNOX. ⎭

MACDUFF.   Confusion now hath made his masterpiece!   67
   Most sacrilegious murder hath broke ope
   The Lord's anointed temple, and stole thence   69
   The life o' the building.

MACBETH.   What is 't you say? The life?

LENNOX.   Mean you his Majesty?

MACDUFF.   Approach the chamber, and destroy your
      sight
   With a new Gorgon. Do not bid me speak;   73
   See, and then speak yourselves.
                         Exeunt MACBETH *and* LENNOX.
                         Awake, awake!
   Ring the alarum bell. Murder and treason!
   Banquo and Donalbain! Malcolm, awake!
   Shake off this downy sleep, death's counterfeit,
   And look on death itself! Up, up, and see
   The great doom's image! Malcolm! Banquo!   79
   As from your graves rise up and walk like sprites   80
   To countenance this horror. Ring the bell.   81
                         Bell rings.

                   Enter LADY MACBETH.

LADY MACBETH.   What's the business,
   That such a hideous trumpet calls to parley   83
   The sleepers of the house? Speak, speak!

MACDUFF.   O gentle lady,
   'Tis not for you to hear what I can speak.
   The repetition in a woman's ear
   Would murder as it fell.

94 **mortality** mortal life

96–97 **The wine . . . vault** a metaphorical passage. The best part
of life (wine) is gone (drawn) and only the dregs (lees) are
left. *Vault* can mean a place where wine is kept, or the
earth, which has an arched (vaulted) sky.

Enter BANQUO.

               O Banquo, Banquo!
Our royal master's murdered.

LADY MACBETH.   Woe, alas!
   What, in our house?

BANQUO.   Too cruel anywhere.
   Dear Duff, I prithee, contradict thyself,
   And say it is not so.

Enter MACBETH *and* LENNOX *and* ROSS.

MACBETH.   Had I but died an hour before this chance,
   I had lived a blessèd time; for from this instant
   There's nothing serious in mortality.   94
   All is but toys; renown and grace is dead;
   The wine of life is drawn, and the mere lees   96
   Is left this vault to brag of.

[margin handwriting: If he had died before no murder]

Enter MALCOLM *and* DONALBAIN.

DONALBAIN.   What is amiss?

MACBETH.   You are, and do not know 't.
   The spring, the head, the fountain of your blood
   Is stopped, the very source of it is stopped.

MACDUFF.   Your royal father's murdered.

MALCOLM.   O, by whom?

LENNOX.   Those of his chamber, as it seemed, had
    done 't.
   Their hands and faces were all badged with blood;
   So were their daggers, which unwiped we found
   Upon their pillows.
   They stared and were distracted. No man's life
   Was to be trusted with them.

MACBETH.   O, yet I do repent me of my fury,
   That I did kill them.

MACDUFF.   Wherefore did you so?

125   **in an augur hole**   in an obscure place. Donalbain is anxious about his and Malcolm's fate, for they may be suspected of the crime.

130   **when . . . hid**   when we have gotten dressed.

MACBETH.   Who can be wise, amazed, temp'rate and
   furious,
Loyal and neutral, in a moment? No man.
Th' expedition of my violent love
Outran the pauser, reason. Here lay Duncan,
His silver skin laced with his golden blood,
And his gashed stabs looked like a breach in nature
For ruin's wasteful entrance; there the murderers,
Steeped in the colors of their trade, their daggers
Unmannerly breeched with gore. Who could refrain,
That had a heart to love, and in that heart
Courage to make 's love known?

LADY MACBETH.   Help me hence, ho!

MALCOLM.   Look to the lady.

MALCOLM.   (*aside to* DONALBAIN) Why do we hold our
   tongues,
That most may claim this argument for ours?

DONALBAIN.   (*aside to* MALCOLM) What should be
   spoken here, where our fate,
Hid in an auger hole, may rush and seize us?   125
Let's away.
Our tears are not yet brewed.

MALCOLM. (*aside to* DONALBAIN) Nor our strong sorrow
Upon the foot of motion.

BANQUO.   Look to the lady.
                         LADY MACBETH *is carried out.*
And when we have our naked frailties hid,   130
That suffer in exposure, let us meet
And question this most bloody piece of work
To know it further. Fears and scruples shake us.
In the great hand of God I stand, and thence
Against the undivulged pretense I fight
Of treasonous malice.

MACDUFF.   And so do I.

69

137   **briefly** quickly.

144–145 **the nearer in blood . . . bloody** the closer their
relationship to the dead king, the more likely it is that they
will be killed.

ALL. So all.

MACBETH.   Let's briefly put on manly readiness,   137
And meet i' the hall together.

ALL. Well contented.
Exeunt all but MALCOLM *and* DONALBAIN.

MALCOLM.   What will you do? Let's not consort with
them.
To show an unfelt sorrow is an office
Which the false man does easy. I'll to England.

DONALBAIN. To Ireland, I. Our separated fortune
Shall keep us both the safer. Where we are,
There's daggers in men's smiles; the nearer in blood,   144
The nearer bloody.

MALCOLM.   This murderous shaft that's shot
Hath not yet lighted, and our safest way
Is to avoid the aim. Therefore to horse,
And let us not be dainty of leave-taking,
But shift away. There's warrant in that theft
Which steals itself when there's no mercy left.
Exeunt.

SCENE 4

Ross and an Old Man talk of recent strange events. When Macduff enters, he tells
Ross that the two servants murdered Duncan and that suspicion falls on Malcolm and
Donalbain, who may have hired the guards to kill the King. Further, Macbeth has
already gone to be invested as King, and Duncan's body has been removed for burial.

Outside Macbeth's castle.
Enter ROSS *with an* OLD MAN.

4   **trifled**   made trivial.

7   **traveling lamp**   the sun.

OLD MAN.   Threescore and ten I can remember well,
   Within the volume of which time I have seen
   Hours dreadful and things strange, but this sore night
   Hath trifled former knowings.

ROSS.   Ha, good father,   4
   Thou seest the heavens, as troubled with man's act,
   Threatens his bloody stage. By th' clock 'tis day,
   And yet dark night strangles the traveling lamp.   7
   Is 't night's predominance, or the day's shame,
   That darkness does the face of earth entomb
   When living light should kiss it?

OLD MAN.   'Tis unnatural,
   Even like the deed that's done. On Tuesday last
   A falcon, towering in her pride of place,
   Was by a mousing owl hawked at and killed.

ROSS   And Duncan's horses—a thing most strange and
      certain—
   Beauteous and swift, the minions of their race,
   Turned wild in nature, broke their stalls, flung out,
   Contending 'gainst obedience, as they would make
   War with mankind.

OLD MAN.   'Tis said they eat each other.

ROSS.   They did so, to th' amazement of mine eyes,
   That looked upon 't.

                Enter MACDUFF.
              Here comes the good Macduff.
   How goes the world, sir, now?

MACDUFF.   Why, see you not?

ROSS.   Is 't known who did this more than bloody deed?

MACDUFF.   Those that Macbeth hath slain.

ROSS.   Alas, the day!
   What good could they pretend?

24   **pretend** intend; **suborned** bribed.

28–29   **Thriftless . . . ravin up . . . life's means** In their wasteful desire to attain the throne, the king's sons have destroyed their very prospect (by running away).

31   **Scone** place where ancient Scottish kings were crowned.

33   **Colmekill** place on the island of Iona where ancient Scottish kings were buried.

36   **Fife** Macduff is Thane of Fife.

40   **benison** blessing.

MACDUFF.   They were suborned.   24
  Malcolm and Donalbain, the King's two sons,
  Are stolen away and fled, which puts upon them
  Suspicion of the deed.

ROSS.   'Gainst nature still!
  Thriftless ambition, that will ravin up   28
  Thine own life's means! Then 'tis most like
  The sovereignty will fall upon Macbeth.

MACDUFF.   He is already named and gone to Scone   31
  To be invested.

ROSS.   Where is Duncan's body?

MACDUFF.   Carried to Colmekill.   33
  The sacred storehouse of his predecessors
  And guardian of their bones.

ROSS.   Will you to Scone?

MACDUFF.   No, cousin, I'll to Fife.

ROSS.   Well, I will thither.   36

MACDUFF.   Well, may you see things well done there.
  Adieu!
  Lest our old robes sit easier than our new!

ROSS.   Farewell, father.

OLD MAN.   God's benison go with you, and with those   40
  That would make good of bad and friends of foes!
                              Exeunt omnes.

MACBETH

ACT III

"The moment on 't, for 't must be done tonight."

s.d.   **sennet**   trumpet call used for ceremonial or formal
          entrances and exits.

13   **all-thing**   in every way.

SCENE 1

At Forres, Banquo muses on Macbeth's successes and wonders if the witches'
prophecies will come true for him as well. Macbeth learns that Banquo and Fleance
will be riding that afternoon. When they have gone, Macbeth sends for two murderers,
whom he instructs to kill both Banquo and Fleance.

Forres. The palace.

Enter BANQUO.

BANQUO.   Thou hast it now—King, Cawdor, Glamis,
   all,
As the weird women promised, and I fear
Thou play'dst most foully for 't. Yet it was said
It should not stand in thy posterity,
But that myself should be the root and father
Of many kings. If there come truth from them—
As upon thee, Macbeth, their speeches shine—
Why, by the verities on thee made good,
May they not be my oracles as well
And set me up in hope? But hush, no more.

Sennet sounded. Enter MACBETH, *as King;* LADY
   MACBETH *as* Queen; LENNOX, ROSS, LORDS,
   and ATTENDANTS.

MACBETH.   Here's our chief guest.

LADY MACBETH.   If he had been forgotten,
   It had been as a gap in our great feast,
   And all-thing unbecoming.

MACBETH.   Tonight we hold a solemn supper, sir,
   And I'll request your presence.

BANQUO.   Let your Highness
   Command upon me, to the which my duties
   Are with a most indissoluble tie
   Forever knit.

MACBETH.   Ride you this afternoon?

n

13

30–31   **bloody cousins are bestowed . . . Ireland**   Malcolm and Donalbain are housed in England and in Ireland.

33   **strange invention**   false stories (accusing Macbeth of murder).

34–35   **cause of state . . . jointly**   affairs of state requiring the attention of both of us.

45   **Sirrah**   (sir'ə) a term used to address male servants, inferiors, and sometimes children.

47   **without**   outside.

BANQUO.   Ay, my good lord.

MACBETH.   We should have else desired your good
   advice,
   Which still hath been both grave and prosperous,
   In this day's council; but we'll take tomorrow.
   Is 't far you ride?

BANQUO.   As far, my lord, as will fill up the time
   'Twixt this and supper. Go not my horse the better,
   I must become a borrower of the night
   For a dark hour or twain.

MACBETH.   Fail not our feast.

BANQUO.   My lord, I will not.

MACBETH.   We hear our bloody cousins are bestowed   30
   In England and in Ireland, not confessing
   Their cruel parricide, filling their hearers
   With strange invention. But of that tomorrow,   33
   When therewithal we shall have cause of state   34
   Craving us jointly. Hie you to horse. Adieu,
   Till you return at night. Goes Fleance with you?

BANQUO.   Ay, my good lord. Our time does call upon 's.

MACBETH.   I wish your horses swift and sure of foot,
   And so I do commend you to their backs.
   Farewell.
                         Exit BANQUO.

Let every man be master of his time
Till seven at night. To make society
The sweeter welcome, we will keep ourself
Till suppertime alone. While then, God be with you!
       Exeunt Lords and all but MACBETH *and a* SERVANT.
Sirrah, a word with you. Attend those men   45
Our pleasure?

SERVANT.   They are, my lord, without the palace gate.   47

48   **thus**   that is, king.

56   **My genius is rebuked**   My guardian spirit (which influences my destiny) is daunted.

65   **filed**   defiled.

68–69   **eternal jewel . . . given . . . common enemy**   given his immortal soul to Satan (the common enemy).

71   **list**   the lists, place of combat.

72   **champion . . . utterance**   fight me to the death.

MACBETH.   Bring them before us.

Exit SERVANT.

To be thus is nothing,   48

But to be safely thus. Our fears in Banquo
Stick deep, and in his royalty of nature
Reigns that which would be feared. 'Tis much he
   dares,
And to that dauntless temper of his mind
He hath a wisdom that doth guide his valor
To act in safety. There is none but he
Whose being I do fear; and under him
My genius is rebuked, as it is said   56
Mark Antony's was by Caesar. He chid the sisters
When first they put the name of king upon me,
And bade them speak to him. Then prophetlike,
They hailed him father to a line of kings.
Upon my head they placed a fruitless crown
And put a barren scepter in my gripe,
Thence to be wrenched with an unlineal hand,
No son of mine succeeding. If 't be so,
For Banquo's issue have I filed my mind;   65
For them the gracious Duncan have I murdered;
Put rancors in the vessel of my peace
Only for them, and mine eternal jewel   68
Given to the common enemy of man
To make them kings, the seeds of Banquo kings!
Rather than so, come, fate, into the list,   71
And champion me to th' utterance! Who's there?   72

Enter SERVANT and two MURDERERS.

Now go to the door, and stay there till we call.

Exit SERVANT.

Was it not yesterday we spoke together?

FIRST MURDERER.   It was, so please your Highness.

80 **passed in probation** went over the evidence.

81 **borne in hand** deluded.

83 **half a soul ... notion crazed** a half wit and a crazed mind.

88 **gospeled** full of the teachings of the Gospels (first four books of the New Testament).

91 **yours** your family.

94 **Shoughs, water-rugs ... demi-wolves** Shaggy dogs, water dogs, and a dog crossbred with a wolf; **clept** called.

95 **file** list

MACBETH.   Well then, now
   Have you considered of my speeches? Know
   That it was he in the times past which held you
   So under fortune, which your thought had been
   Our innocent self. This I made good to you
   In our last conference, passed in probation with you   80
   How you were borne in hand, how crossed, the   81
      instruments,
   Who wrought with them, and all things else that
      might
   To half a soul and to a notion crazed   83
   Say "Thus did Banquo."

FIRST MURDERER.   You made it known to us.

MACBETH.   I did so; and went further, which is now
   Our point of second meeting. Do you find
   Your patience so predominant in your nature
   That you can let this go? Are you so gospeled   88
   To pray for this good man and for his issue,
   Whose heavy hand hath bowed you to the grave
   And beggared yours for ever?   91

FIRST MURDERER.   We are men, my liege.

MACBETH.   Ay, in the catalogue ye go for men,
   As hounds and greyhounds, mongrels, spaniels, curs,
   Shoughs, water-rugs, and demi-wolves, are clept   94
   All by the name of dogs. The valued file   95
   Distinguishes the swift, the slow, the subtle,
   The housekeeper, the hunter, every one
   According to the gift which bounteous nature
   Hath in him closed, whereby he does receive
   Particular addition, from the bill
   That writes them all alike; and so of men.
   Now, if you have a station in the file,
   Not i' the worst rank of manhood, say 't,
   And I will put that business in your bosoms
   Whose execution takes your enemy off,
   Grapples you to the heart and love of us,

116–118 **distance**   space to be kept between fencers. Banquo is too close. The fencing metaphor is continued through the first part of line 118; **near'st of life**   most vital part.

120   **bid my will avouch it**   justify his death by my wish only.

124   **to . . . make love**   try to get your assistance or woo your help.

130   **spy o' the time**   Macbeth might mean that eventually he will tell the murderers the time to begin looking for Banquo.

133   **I require a clearness**   I do not want suspicion to fall on me.

Who wear our health but sickly in his life,
Which in his death were perfect.

SECOND MURDERER.   I am one, my liege,
Whom the vile blows and buffets of the world
Have so incensed that I am reckless what
I do to spite the world.

FIRST MURDERER.   And I another,
So weary with disasters, tugged with fortune,
That I would set my life on any chance
To mend it or be rid on 't.

MACBETH.   Both of you
Know Banquo was your enemy.

BOTH MURDERERS.   True, my lord.

MACBETH.   So is he mine, and in such bloody distance   116
That every minute of his being thrusts
Against my near'st of life: and though I could
With barefaced power sweep him from my sight
And bid my will avouch it, yet I must not,   120
For certain friends that are both his and mine,
Whose loves I may not drop, but wail his fall
Who I myself struck down. And thence it is
That I to your assistance do make love,   124
Masking the business from the common eye
For sundry weighty reasons.

SECOND MURDERER.   We shall, my lord,
Perform what you command us.

FIRST MURDERER.   Though our lives—

MACBETH.   Your spirits shine through you. Within this
   hour at most
I will advise you where to plant yourselves,
Acquaint you with the perfect spy o' the time,   130
The moment on 't, for 't must be done tonight,
And something from the palace; always thought
That I require a clearness; and with him—   133
To leave no rubs nor botches in the work—
Fleance his son, that keeps him company,

138   **Resolve yourselves apart**   meet privately to make up your minds.

Whose absence is no less material to me
Than is his father's, must embrace the fate
Of that dark hour. Resolve yourselves apart;   138
I'll come to you anon.

BOTH MURDERERS.   We are resolved, my lord.

MACBETH.   I'll call upon you straight. Abide within.

               Exeunt MURDERERS.

It is concluded. Banquo, thy soul's flight,
If it find heaven, must find it out tonight.

                    Exit.

SCENE 2

Before the great banquet begins, Lady Macbeth urges Macbeth to forget what is past and be jovial. Macbeth asks that she be the same and honor Banquo particularly. He hints, however, that a dreadful deed will be done, and when she questions him, he replies that she should not know until later.

The palace.

Enter LADY MACBETH *and a* SERVANT.

LADY MACBETH.   Is Banquo gone from court?

SERVANT.   Ay, madam, but returns again tonight.

LADY MACBETH.   Say to the King I would attend his leisure
For a few words.

SERVANT.   Madam, I will.

                    Exit.

13   **scorched**   slashed.

16   **both the worlds suffer**   heaven and earth perish.

32–33   **Unsafe . . . streams**   Because we are unsafe now, we must wash (lave) our honors in streams of flattery to make our honors seem clean.

34   **vizards**   masks.

LADY MACBETH.   Naught 's had, all 's
    spent,
  Where our desire is got without content.
  'Tis safer to be that which we destroy
  Than by destruction dwell in doubtful joy.

                  Enter MACBETH.
  How now, my lord! Why do you keep alone,
  Of sorriest fancies your companions making,
  Using those thoughts which should indeed have died
  With them they think on? Things without all remedy
  Should be without regard. What's done is done.

MACBETH.   We have scorched the snake, not killed it.   13
  She'll close and be herself, whilst our poor malice
  Remains in danger of her former tooth.
  But let the frame of things disjoint, both the worlds
      suffer,   16
  Ere we will eat our meal in fear and sleep
  In the affliction of these terrible dreams
  That shake us nightly. Better be with the dead,
  Whom we, to gain our peace, have sent to peace,
  Than on the torture of the mind to lie
  In restless ecstasy. Duncan is in his grave;
  After life's fitful fever he sleeps well.
  Treason has done his worst; nor steel, nor poison,
  Malice domestic, foreign levy, nothing,
  Can touch him further.

LADY MACBETH.   Come on,
  Gentle my lord, sleek o'er your rugged looks;
  Be bright and jovial among your guests tonight.

MACBETH.   So shall I, love; and so, I pray, be you.
  Let your remembrance apply to Banquo;
  Present him eminence, both with eye and tongue—
  Unsafe the while, that we   32
  Must lave our honors in these flattering streams
  And make our faces vizards to our hearts,   34
  Disguising what they are.

38   **nature's copy's not eterne**   Nature has granted Banquo and Fleance only a lease on life, not perpetual life. (A *copyhold* is a kind of lease.)

40   **jocund**   joyful.

46   **seeling**   blinding. The reference is to the practice of sewing up (seeling) the eyes of falcons to make them tame.

47   **scarf up**   blindfold.

LADY MACBETH.　　　　　You must leave this.

MACBETH.　O, full of scorpions is my mind, dear wife!
　Thou know'st that Banquo, and his Fleance, lives.

LADY MACBETH.　But in them nature's copy's not
　　eterne.　　　　　　　　　　　　　　　　　　　　38

MACBETH.　There's comfort yet; they are assailable.
　Then be thou jocund. Ere the bat hath flown　　　40
　His cloistered flight, ere to black Hecate's summons
　The shard-borne beetle with his drowsy hums
　Hath rung night's yawning peal, there shall be done
　A deed of dreadful note.

LADY MACBETH.　　　　　What's to be done?

MACBETH.　Be innocent of the knowledge, dearest
　　chuck,
　Till thou applaud the deed. Come, seeling night,　　46
　Scarf up the tender eye of pitiful day.　　　　　　47
　And with thy bloody and invisible hand
　Cancel and tear to pieces that great bond
　Which keeps me pale! Light thickens, and the crow
　Makes wing to th' rooky wood:
　Good things of day begin to droop and drowse,
　Whiles night's black agents to their preys do rouse.
　Thou marvel'st at my words, but hold thee still;
　Things bad begun make strong themselves by ill.
　So, prithee, go with me.

　　　　　　　　　　　　　　Exeunt.

Macbeth wants prophesy to be true. and False [handwritten annotation]

SCENE 3

*The two murderers, now joined by a third, wait near the palace for the return of
Banquo and Fleance. They murder Banquo, but Fleance escapes.*

2–4   **He . . . just**   We needn't mistrust him (the third murderer), since he has given us the same directions that Macbeth gave us. There are various theories as to why a third murderer was introduced at this point, the most likely being that it takes two people to carry Banquo's body offstage and a third to pick up the dropped torch before the start of the banquet scene.

11–14   **go about . . . walk**   take the long way to the castle and walk to the gate. (This eliminates the need for horses onstage.)

A park near the palace.

Enter three MURDERERS.

FIRST MURDERER.   But who did bid thee join with us?

THIRD MURDERER.   Macbeth.

SECOND MURDERER.   He needs not our mistrust, since
    he delivers   2
Our offices, and what we have to do,
To the direction just.

FIRST MURDERER.   Then stand with us.
The west yet glimmers with some streaks of day.
Now spurs the lated traveler apace
To gain the timely inn, and near approaches
The subject of our watch.

THIRD MURDERER.   Hark! I hear horses.

BANQUO.   (*within*) Give us a light there, ho!

SECOND MURDERER.   Then 'tis he. The rest
That are within the note of expectation
Already are i' the court.

FIRST MURDERER.   His horses go about.   11

THIRD MURDERER.   Almost a mile; but he does usually—
So all men do—from hence to the palace gate
Make it their walk.

    Enter BANQUO, *and* FLEANCE *with a torch.*

SECOND MURDERER.   A light, a light!

THIRD MURDERER.   'Tis he.

FIRST MURDERER.   Stand to 't.

BANQUO.   It will be rain tonight.

FIRST MURDERER.   Let it come down!
                 They set upon BANQUO.

20   **way**   thing to do.

1   **degrees**   ranks. Guests were seated according to rank.

BANQUO.   O, treachery! Fly, good Fleance, fly, fly, fly!
Thou mayst revenge. O slave!

BANQUO dies. FLEANCE escapes.

THIRD MURDERER.   Who did strike out the light?

FIRST MURDERER.   Was 't not the way?   20

THIRD MURDERER.   There's but one down; the son is
fled.

SECOND MURDERER.   We have lost.
Best half of our affair.

FIRST MURDERER.   Well, let's away and say how much is
done.

Exeunt.

SCENE 4

One of the murderers reports to Macbeth, who is disturbed by the news that Fleance is still alive. When Macbeth goes into the banquet, he discovers Banquo's ghost sitting in his place. To the assembled lords, Lady Macbeth tries to make light of Macbeth's reactions. Privately, she tells Macbeth that he is imagining things. When the ghost appears and disappears a second time, she dismisses the guests. Macbeth now vows to send for Macduff and to visit the witches.

Hall in the palace.

Banquet prepared. Enter MACBETH, LADY MACBETH,
ROSS, LENNOX, LORDS, and ATTENDANTS.

MACBETH.   You know your own degrees; sit down. At
first   1
And last the hearty welcome.

LORDS.   Thanks to your Majesty.

97

14   **'Tis better . . . within**   It's better for the blood to be on you than in him.

19   **nonpareil**   without equal.

23   **casing**   enveloping.

25   **saucy**   sharp.

MACBETH.   Ourself will mingle with society
And play the humble host.
Our hostess keeps her state, but in best time
We will require her welcome.

LADY MACBETH.   Pronounce it for me, sir, to all our
friends,
For my heart speaks they are welcome.

Enter FIRST MURDERER *to the door.*
MACBETH.   See, they encounter thee with their hearts'
thanks.
Both sides are even. Here I'll sit i' the midst.
Be large in mirth; anon we'll drink a measure
The table round. (*He goes to the door.*) There's blood
upon thy face.

MURDERER.   'Tis Banquo's then.

MACBETH.   'Tis better thee without than he within.   14
Is he dispatched?

MURDERER.   My lord, his throat is cut. That I did for
him.

MACBETH.   Thou art the best o' the cutthroats. Yet he's
good
That did the like for Fleance. If thou didst it,
Thou art the nonpareil.

MURDERER.   Most royal sir,   19
Fleance is 'scaped.

MACBETH.   (*aside*) Then comes my fit again. I had else
been perfect,
Whole as the marble, founded as the rock,
As broad and general as the casing air.   23
But now I am cabined, cribbed, confined, bound in
To saucy doubts and fears.—But Banquo's safe?   25

MURDERER.   Ay, my good lord; safe in a ditch he bides,
With twenty trenchèd gashes on his head,
The least a death to nature.

32   **We'll hear . . . again**   We'll confer.

33–36   **You . . . ceremony**   It seems as if the feast is given for payment unless the guests are repeatedly assured that they are welcome. Mere eating is best done at home. Away, courtesy (ceremony) flavors the food.

40–41   **Here . . . roofed . . . present**   If Banquo were here, all Scotland's noblemen would be under one roof.

42–43   **I . . . mischance**   I would rather blame him for unkindness [in not attending] than pity him in case he had an accident.

MACBETH. Thanks for that.
There the grown serpent lies; the worm that 's fled
Hath nature that in time will venom breed,
No teeth for th' present. Get thee gone. Tomorrow
We'll hear ourselves again.

Exit MURDERER.

LADY MACBETH. My royal lord, 32
You do not give the cheer. The feast is sold 33
That is not often vouched, while 'tis a making,
'Tis given with welcome. To feed were best at home;
From thence, the sauce to meat is ceremony;
Meeting were bare without it.

Enter the GHOST *of* BANQUO, *who sits in* MACBETH'S *place.*
MACBETH. Sweet remembrancer!
Now good digestion wait on appetite,
And health on both!

LENNOX. May 't please your highness sit.

MACBETH. Here had we now our country's honor
roofed, 40
Were the graced person of our Banquo present;
Who may I rather challenge for unkindness 42
Than pity for mischance.

ROSS. His absence, sir,
Lays blame upon his promise. Please 't your Highness
To grace us with your royal company?

MACBETH. The table's full.

LENNOX. Here is a place reserved, sir.

MACBETH. Where?

LENNOX. Here, my good lord. What is 't that moves
your Highness?

MACBETH. Which of you have done this?

LORDS. What, my good lord?

60 **O, proper stuff!** O, nonsense!

71 **charnel houses** storehouses for the bones of the dead.

72–73 **monuments . . . maws of kites** our only monuments will be the stomachs (maws) of kites, scavenging birds.

MACBETH.   Thou canst not say I did it. Never shake
   Thy gory locks at me.

ROSS.   Gentlemen, rise. His Highness is not well.

LADY MACBETH.   Sit, worthy friends. My lord is often
      thus,
   And hath been from his youth. Pray you, keep seat.
   The fit is momentary; upon a thought
   He will again be well. If much you note him,
   You shall offend him and extend his passion.
   Feed, and regard him not. (*Apart with* MACBETH.) Are
      you a man?

MACBETH.   Ay, and a bold one, that dare look on that
   Which might appall the devil.

LADY MACBETH.   O, proper stuff!   60
   This is the very painting of your fear.
   This is the air-drawn dagger which, you said,
   Led you to Duncan. O, these flaws and starts,
   Impostors to true fear, would well become
   A woman's story at a winter's fire,
   Authorized by her grandam. Shame itself!
   Why do you make such faces? When all's done,
   You look but on a stool.

MACBETH.   Prithee, see there! Behold! Look! Lo! How
      say you?
   Why, what care I? If thou canst nod, speak too.
   If charnel houses and our graves must send   71
   Those that we bury back, our monuments   72
   Shall be the maws of kites.

                              Exit GHOST.

LADY MACBETH.   What, quite unmanned in folly?

MACBETH.   If I stand here, I saw him.

LADY MACBETH.   Fie, for shame!

76 **Ere humane statute . . . weal** before humane, or human, law cleansed society of violence.

81 **mortal murders** deadly wounds.

93 **Avaunt** Go away!

101 **Hyrcan tiger** tiger from Hyrcania, formerly a region south of the Caspian Sea.

MACBETH.   Blood hath been shed ere now, i' th' olden
    time,
  Ere humane statute purged the gentle weal;   76
  Ay, and since too, murders have been performed
  Too terrible for the ear. The time has been
  That, when the brains were out, the man would die,
  And there an end; but now they rise again,
  With twenty mortal murders on their crowns,   81
  And push us from our stools. This is more strange
  Than such a murder is.

LADY MACBETH.   My worthy lord,
  Your noble friends do lack you.

MACBETH.   I do forget.
  Do not muse at me, my most worthy friends;
  I have a strange infirmity, which is nothing
  To those that know me. Come, love and health to all!
  Then I'll sit down. Give me some wine; fill full.
              Enter GHOST.
  I drink to the general joy o' th' whole table,
  And to our dear friend Banquo, whom we miss.
  Would he were here! To all, and him, we thirst,
  And all to all.

LORDS.   Our duties, and the pledge.

MACBETH.   (*to the* GHOST)   Avaunt and quit my sight!
  Let the earth hide thee!   93
  Thy bones are marrowless, thy blood is cold;
  Thou hast no speculation in those eyes
  Which thou dost glare with.

LADY MACBETH.   Think of this, good peers,
  But as a thing of custom. 'Tis no other;
  Only it spoils the pleasure of the time.

MACBETH.   What man dare, I dare.
  Approach thou like the rugged Russian bear,
  The armed rhinoceros, or the Hyrcan tiger;   101
  Take any shape but that, and my firm nerves
  Shall never tremble. Or be alive again,
  And dare me to the desert with thy sword.

105–106 **If . . . girl**   If then I live in terror, call me a baby girl.

110   **admired disorder**   deranged behavior that caused
          astonishment.

123–126 **Stones . . . blood**   Stones and trees, as well as magpies,
          choughs, and rooks (all birds that can be taught to talk),
          have been known to reveal a murderer.

If trembling I inhabit then, protest me   105
The baby of a girl. Hence, horrible shadow!
Unreal mockery, hence!

Exit GHOST.

Why, so; being gone,
I am a man again. Pray you, sit still.

LADY MACBETH.   You have displaced the mirth, broke
the good meeting,
With most admired disorder.

MACBETH.   Can such things be,   110
And overcome us like a summer's cloud,
Without our special wonder? You make me strange
Even to the disposition that I owe,
When now I think you can behold such sights,
And keep the natural ruby of your cheeks.
When mine is blanched with fear.

ROSS.   What sights, my lord?

LADY MACBETH.   I pray you, speak not. He grows worse
and worse;
Question enrages him. At once, good night.
Stand not upon the order of your going,
But go at once.

LENNOX.   Good night, and better health
Attend his Majesty!

LADY MACBETH.   A kind good night to all!

Exeunt LORDS *and* ATTENDANTS.

MACBETH.   It will have blood, they say; blood will have
blood.
Stones have been known to move and trees to speak;   123
Augurs and understood relations have
By maggotpies and choughs and rooks brought forth
The secret'st man of blood. What is the night?

LADY MACBETH.   Almost at odds with morning, which is
which.

131–132 **There's not a one of them . . . servant fee'd** He pays
servants to spy in the noblemen's houses.

142   **self-abuse**   self-delusion.

MACBETH.   How say'st thou, that Macduff denies his person
At our great bidding?

LADY MACBETH,   Did you send to him, sir?

MACBETH.   I hear it by the way; but I will send.
There's not a one of them but in his house   131
I keep a servant fee'd. I will tomorrow—
And betimes I will—to the Weird Sisters.
More shall they speak, for now I am bent to know
By the worst means the worst. For mine own good
All causes shall give way. I am in blood
Stepped in so far that, should I wade no more,
Returning were as tedious as go o'er.
Strange things I have in head, that will to hand,
Which must be acted ere they may be scanned.

LADY MACBETH.   You lack the season of all natures, sleep.

MACBETH.   Come, we'll to sleep. My strange and self-abuse   142
Is the initiate fear that wants hard use.
We are yet but young in deed.

                                        Exeunt.

SCENE 5

Hecate chides the witches because she has not been consulted about their dealings with Macbeth, and she advises them to prepare more spells for his return.

A heath.

Thunder. Enter the three WITCHES, *meeting* HECATE.

FIRST WITCH.   Why, how now, Hecate! You look angerly.

2   **beldams**   hags. Some editors punctuate lines 2 and 3 as follows: . . . beldams as you are?/Saucy and overbold, how did you dare . . . ?

15   **Acheron**   In Greek mythology, a river in Hades, the underworld, but meant figuratively here because in Act IV Macbeth meets them in a Scottish cavern.

HECATE.   Have I not reason, beldams as you are,   2
   Saucy and overbold? How did you dare
   To trade and traffic with Macbeth
   In riddles and affairs of death;
   And I, the mistress of your charms,
   The close contriver of all harms,
   Was never called to bear my part
   Or show the glory of our art?
   And, which is worse, all you have done
   Hath been but for a wayward son,
   Spiteful and wrathful, who, as others do,
   Loves for his own ends, not for you.
   But make amends now. Get you gone,
   And at the pit of Acheron   15
   Meet me i' the morning. Thither he
   Will come to know his destiny.
   Your vessels and your spells provide,
   Your charms and every thing beside.
   I am for th' air. This night I'll spend
   Unto a dismal and a fatal end.
   Great business must be wrought ere noon.
   Upon the corner of the moon
   There hangs a vaporous drop profound;
   I'll catch it ere it comes to ground,
   And that, distilled by magic sleights
   Shall raise such artificial sprites
   As by the strength of their illusion
   Shall draw him on to his confusion.
   He shall spurn fate, scorn death, and bear
   His hopes 'bove wisdom, grace, and fear.
   And you all know, security
   Is mortals' chiefest enemy.

   Music and a song within: "Come away, come away," etc.

   Hark! I am called. My little spirit, see,
   Sits in a foggy cloud, and stays for me.
                Exit.

FIRST WITCH.   Come, let's make haste. She'll soon be
   back again.
                Exeunt.

1   **former speeches . . . thoughts**   What I have said has matched your thoughts.

3   **borne**   managed.

4   **of**   by; **marry, he was dead**   Lennox means that Macbeth pitied Duncan only after he was dead.

21   **broad words**   plain speaking.

22   **tyrant's feast**   Macbeth's feast

SCENE 6

Lennox and another lord talk of their suspicions about the death of Duncan and Banquo and express the hope that the English king will send help.

Forres. Near the palace.

Enter LENNOX *and another* LORD.

LENNOX.   My former speeches have but hit your
   thoughts,   1
Which can interpret farther. Only I say
Things have been strangely borne. The gracious
   Duncan   3
Was pitied of Macbeth; marry, he was dead.   4
And the right-valiant Banquo walked too late;
Whom, you may say, if 't please you, Fleance killed,
For Fleance fled. Men must not walk too late.
Who cannot want the thought, how monstrous
It was for Malcolm and for Donalbain
To kill their gracious father? Damnèd fact!
How it did grieve Macbeth! Did he not straight
In pious rage the two delinquents tear,
That were the slaves of drink and thralls of sleep?
Was not that nobly done? Ay, and wisely too;
For 'twould have angered any heart alive
To hear the men deny 't. So that I say,
He has borne all things well; and I do think
That, had he Duncan's sons under his key—
As, an 't please heaven, he shall not—they should
   find
What 'twere to kill a father. So should Fleance.
But, peace! For from broad words, and 'cause he failed   21
His presence at the tyrant's feast, I hear   22
Macduff lives in disgrace. Sir, can you tell
Where he bestows himself?

27 **Edward** Edward the Confessor, the English king.

31 **wake Northumberland . . . Siward** call the people of Northumberland to arms. Siward is the Earl of Northumberland.

38 **the King** Macbeth.

40–43 **He did . . . answer.** Macbeth sent a messenger to summon Macduff, who sent the messenger back with a refusal. The scowling messenger implies that Macduff will be sorry he refused. (The *me* in line 41 is dialect and does not refer to the lord who is speaking.)

LORD.   The son of Duncan,
From whom this tyrant holds the due of birth,
Lives in the English court, and is received
Of the most pious Edward with such grace   27
That the malevolence of fortune nothing
Takes from his high respect. Thither Macduff
Is gone to pray the holy king, upon his aid
To wake Northumberland and warlike Siward,   31
That by the help of these, with Him above
To ratify the work, we may again
Give to our tables meat, sleep to our nights,
Free from our feasts and banquets bloody knives,
Do faithful homage and receive free honors—
All which we pine for now. And this report
Hath so exasperate the King that he   38
Prepares for some attempt of war.

LENNOX.   Sent he to Macduff?

LORD.   He did; and with an absolute "Sir not I,"   40
The cloudy messenger turns me his back,
And hums, as who should say "You'll rue the time
That clogs me with this answer."

LENNOX.   And that well might
Advise him to a caution, t' hold what distance
His wisdom can provide. Some holy angel
Fly to the court of England and unfold
His message ere he come, that a swift blessing
May soon return to this our suffering country
Under a hand accursed!

LORD.   I'll send my prayers with him.
                                        Exeunt.

ACT IV

"Be not found here. Hence with your little ones!"

1   **Thrice** three times.

2   **hedgepig** hedgehog, a small mammal with a shaggy coat and sharp spines, somewhat like a porcupine.

3   **Harpier** the third witch's familiar spirit. The word may be derived from *harpy*, in Greek myth a bird with the head of a woman.

6–8   **Toad . . . sweltered venom . . . got** toad that sweated (sweltered) venom for thirty-one days and nights while sleeping.

12   **fenny snake** snake that lives in a marsh or fen.

17   **howlet** small owl.

23   **witches' mummy** mummified human flesh; **maw and gulf** stomach and gullet.

24   **ravined** ravenous.

SCENE 1

Macbeth revisits the witches and demands to know more than they have told him thus far. Three apparitions appear and prophesy. A procession of eight kings appears as well, followed by Banquo's ghost. Lennox appears to tell Macbeth that Macduff has gone to England, and Macbeth resolves to seize Macduff's castle and kill his wife and children.

A cavern. In the middle, a boiling cauldron.

Thunder. Enter the three WITCHES.

FIRST WITCH.   Thrice the brinded cat hath mewed.   1

SECOND WITCH.   Thrice and once the hedgepig whined.   2

THIRD WITCH.   Harpier cries " 'Tis time, 'tis time."   3

FIRST WITCH. Round about the cauldron go;
In the poisoned entrails throw.
Toad, that under cold stone   6
Days and nights has thirty-one
Sweltered venom sleeping got,
Boil thou first i' the charmèd pot.

ALL.   Double, double, toil and trouble;
Fire burn and cauldron bubble.

SECOND WITCH.   Fillet of a fenny snake,   12
In the cauldron boil and bake;
Eye of newt and toe of frog,
Wool of bat and tongue of dog,
Adder's fork and blindworm's sting,
Lizard's leg and howlet's wing,   17
For a charm of powerful trouble,
Like a hell-broth boil and bubble.

ALL.   Double, double, toil and trouble;
Fire burn and cauldron bubble.

THIRD WITCH.   Scale of dragon, tooth of wolf,
Witches' mummy, maw and gulf   23
Of the ravined salt-sea shark,   24
Root of hemlock digged i' the dark,

27 **yew** tree thought to be poisonous.

28 **slivered . . . eclipse** cut off when the moon is in eclipse, a time thought to be ominous.

31 **Ditch-delivered . . . drab** delivered in a ditch by a whore.

33 **chaudron** entrails.

53 **yesty** yeasty, foamy.

Liver of blaspheming Jew,
Gall of goat and slips of yew   27
Slivered in the moon's eclipse,   28
Nose of Turk and Tartar's lips,
Finger of birth-strangled babe
Ditch-delivered by a drab,   31
Make the gruel thick and slab.
Add thereto a tiger's chaudron   33
For th' ingredients of our cauldron.

ALL.   Double, double, toil and trouble;
Fire burn, and cauldron bubble.

SECOND WITCH.   Cool it with a baboon's blood,
Then the charm is firm and good.

Enter HECATE *to the other three* WITCHES.
HECATE.   O, well done! I commend your pains,
And every one shall share i' the gains.
And now about the cauldron sing
Like elves and fairies in a ring,
Enchanting all that you put in.

Music and a song: "Black spirits," etc. Exit HECATE.

SECOND WITCH.   By the pricking of my thumbs,
Something wicked this way comes.
Open, locks,
Whoever knocks!

Enter MACBETH.
MACBETH.   How now, you secret, black, and midnight
hags!
What is 't you do?

ALL.   A deed without a name.

MACBETH.   I conjure you, by that which you profess,
Howe'er you come to know it, answer me.
Though you untie the winds and let them fight
Against the churches; though the yesty waves   53
Confound and swallow navigation up;
Though bladed corn be lodged and trees blown down;

59 **nature's germins**   the seeds, or basic elements, of everything in nature.

65–66 **grease ... gibbet**   grease made from the sweat of a murderer hung from a gallows.

68 **office**   function.

s.d. **armed Head**   This might symbolize Macbeth's head, but he may believe that it represents Macduff's head.

Though castles topple on their warders' heads;
Though palaces and pyramids do slope
Their heads to their foundations; though the treasure
Of nature's germins tumble all together,   59
Even till destruction sickens—answer me
To what I ask you.

FIRST WITCH.   Speak.

SECOND WITCH.   Demand.

THIRD WITCH.   We'll answer.

FIRST WITCH.   Say, if thou'dst rather hear it from our mouths
Or from our masters?

MACBETH.   Call 'em. Let me see 'em.

FIRST WITCH.   Pour in sow's blood, that hath eaten
Her nine farrow; grease that's sweaten   65
From the murderer's gibbet throw
Into the flame.

ALL.   Come high or low;
Thyself and office deftly show!   68

    Thunder. FIRST APPARITION, *an armed Head.*   n

MACBETH.   Tell me, thou unknown power—

FIRST WITCH.   He knows thy thought.
Hear his speech, but say thou naught.

FIRST APPARITION.   Macbeth! Macbeth! Macbeth!
Beware Macduff;
Beware the Thane of Fife. Dismiss me. Enough.

              He descends.

MACBETH.   Whate'er thou art, for thy good caution thanks;
Thou hast harped my fear aright. But one word more—

FIRST WITCH.   He will not be commanded. Here's another,
More potent than the first.

s.d.   **bloody Child**   This may represent Macduff. See Act V,
Scene 8, lines 15–16.

83–84   **But yet . . . bond of fate**   By killing Macduff, Macbeth will
get a guarantee from fate that Macduff won't harm him.

s.d.   **a Child crowned . . . hand**   the crowned child symbolizes
Malcolm, and the tree may symbolize the branches of
Birnam Wood.

96   **bodements**   prophecies.

97   **Rebellion's head**   Some critics think this should read
"Rebellious dead." "Rebellion's head" may refer to an
armed uprising; "Rebellious dead," to Banquo and his
descendants.

Thunder. SECOND APPARITION, *a bloody Child.*   n

SECOND APPARITION. Macbeth! Macbeth! Macbeth!

MACBETH.   Had I three ears, I'd hear thee.

SECOND APPARITION.   Be bloody, bold, and resolute;
laugh to scorn
The power of man, for none of woman born
Shall harm Macbeth.

Descends.

MACBETH.   Then live, Macduff; what need I fear of
thee?
But yet I'll make assurance doubly sure,   83
And take a bond of fate. Thou shalt not live,
That I may tell pale-hearted fear it lies,
And sleep in spite of thunder.

Thunder. THIRD APPARITION, *a Child crowned, with a*
tree in his hand.   n

What is this
That rises like the issue of a king
And wears upon his baby brow the round
And top of sovereignty?

ALL.   Listen, but speak not to 't.

THIRD APPARITION.   Be lion-mettled, proud, and take
no care
Who chafes, who frets, or where conspirers are.
Macbeth shall never vanquished be until
Great Birnam Wood to high Dunsinane Hill
Shall come against him.

Descends.

MACBETH.   That will never be.
Who can impress the forest, bid the tree
Unfix his earth-bound root? Sweet bodements, good!   96
Rebellion's head, rise never till the wood   97
Of Birnam rise, and our high-placed Macbeth
Shall live the lease of nature, pay his breath
To time and mortal custom. Yet my heart

s.d.   **glass**   perhaps a mirror.

120   **two-fold balls and treble scepters**   An orb (ball) and a
         scepter traditionally signify royalty. The orb is a sphere
         topped by a cross. The scepter is an ornamented staff. Both
         are carried on ceremonial occasions, such as a coronation.
         The two-fold ball might refer to King James's double
         kingship of England and Scotland. In 1604 James assumed
         the title of King of Great Britain, France, and Ireland,
         possibly symbolized by the three scepters. Banquo was
         supposedly the founder of the Stuart line of rulers.

Throbs to know one thing. Tell me, if your art
Can tell so much, shall Banquo's issue ever
Reign in this kingdom?

ALL.   Seek to know no more.

MACBETH.   I will be satisfied. Deny me this,
And an eternal curse fall on you! Let me know—

Hautboys.

Why sinks that cauldron? And what noise is this?

FIRST WITCH.   Show!

SECOND WITCH.   Show!

THIRD WITCH.   Show!

ALL.   Show his eyes, and grieve his heart;
Come like shadows, so depart!

A show of eight Kings, and BANQUO, *the last King with a
glass in his hand.*

MACBETH.   Thou art too like the spirit of Banquo.
   Down!
Thy crown does sear mine eyeballs. And thy hair,
Thou other gold-bound brow, is like the first.
A third is like the former. Filthy hags,
Why do you show me this? A fourth? Start, eyes!
What, will the line stretch out to th' crack of doom?
Another yet? A seventh? I'll see no more.
And yet the eighth appears, who bears a glass
Which shows me many more; and some I see
That two-fold balls and treble scepters carry.
Horrible sight! Now I see 'tis true,
For the blood-boltered Banquo smiles upon me
And points at them for his. (APPARITIONS *vanish.*)
   What, is this so?

FIRST WITCH.   Ay, sir, all this is so. But why
Stands Macbeth thus amazedly?
Come, sisters, cheer we up his sprites
And show the best of our delights.

120

129   **antic round**   grotesque round dance.

144–145 **flighty purpose . . . go with it**   Purpose is fleeting and will never be achieved unless action accompanies thought.

I'll charm the air to give a sound,
While you perform your antic round,   129
That this great king may kindly say
Our duties did his welcome pay.
                    Music. The WITCHES *dance, and vanish.*

MACBETH.   Where are they? Gone? Let this pernicious
    hour
Stand aye accursèd in the calendar!
Come in, without there!

                    Enter LENNOX.
LENNOX   What's your Grace's will?

MACBETH.   Saw you the Weird Sisters?

LENNOX.   No, my lord.

MACBETH.   Came they not by you?

LENNOX.   No indeed, my lord.

MACBETH.   Infected be the air whereon they ride,
    And damned all those that trust them! I did hear
    The galloping of horse. Who was 't came by?

LENNOX.   'Tis two or three, my lord, that bring you
    word
Macduff is fled to England.

MACBETH.   Fled to England!

LENNOX.   Ay, my good lord.

MACBETH.   (*aside*) Time, thou anticipatest my dread
    exploits.
The flighty purpose never is o'ertook   144
Unless the deed go with it. From this moment
The very firstlings of my heart shall be
The firstlings of my hand. And even now,
To crown my thoughts with acts, be it thought and
    done:
The castle of Macduff I will surprise,
Seize upon Fife, give to th' edge o' the sword
His wife, his babes, and all unfortunate souls

152   **trace . . . line**   follow him in the family succession.

9   **He wants the natural touch**   He lacks the natural feelings that should make him want to protect his family.

That trace him in his line. No boasting like a fool;   152
This deed I'll do before this purpose cool.
But no more sights!—Where are these gentlemen?
Come, bring me where they are.

Exeunt.

SCENE 2

Lady Macduff laments the fact that her husband is gone. She is informed by a messenger that she is in danger and should leave at once. Before she can do so, she and her son are killed.

Fife. Macduff's castle.

Enter LADY MACDUFF, *her* SON, *and* ROSS.

LADY MACDUFF.   What had he done to make him fly
the land?

ROSS.   You must have patience, madam.

LADY MACDUFF.   He had none.
His flight was madness; when our actions do not,
Our fears do make us traitors.

ROSS.   You know not
Whether it was his wisdom or his fear.

LADY MACDUFF.   Wisdom? To leave his wife, to leave
his babes,
His mansion, and his titles in a place
From whence himself does fly? He loves us not;
He wants the natural touch; for the poor wren,   9
The most diminutive of birds, will fight,
Her young ones in her nest, against the owl.
All is the fear and nothing is the love,
As little is the wisdom, where the flight
So runs against all reason.

14   **coz**   cousin, kinswoman.

17   **fits o' the season**   disorders of the times.

18–19   **are traitors . . . ourselves**   are said to be traitors but do not
        know ourselves to be traitors.

29   **It . . . discomfort**   He would disgrace himself by weeping
        and thus embarrass her.

34–35   **lime . . . pitfall . . . gin**   *Lime* is birdlime, a sticky substance
        put on branches to catch birds; a *pitfall* is a snare; a *gin* is a
        trap.

ROSS. My dearest coz, 14
  I pray you, school yourself. But, for your husband,
  He is noble, wise, judicious, and best knows
  The fits o' the season. I dare not speak much further, 17
  But cruel are the times when we are traitors 18
  And do not know ourselves; when we hold rumor
  From what we fear, yet know not what we fear,
  But float upon a wild and violent sea
  Each way and none. I take my leave of you;
  Shall not be long but I'll be here again.
  Things at the worst will cease, or else climb upward
  To what they were before.—My pretty cousin,
  Blessing upon you!

LADY MACDUFF. Fathered he is, and yet he's fatherless.

ROSS. I am so much a fool, should I stay longer,
  It would be my disgrace and your discomfort. 29
  I take my leave at once.

                                   Exit.

LADY MACDUFF. Sirrah, your father's dead;
  And what will you do now? How will you live?

SON. As birds do, Mother.

LADY MACDUFF. What, with worms and flies?

SON. With what I get, I mean; and so do they.

LADY MACDUFF. Poor bird! Thou'dst never fear the net
    nor lime, 34
  The pitfall nor the gin.

SON. Why should I, Mother? Poor birds they are not
    set for.
  My father is not dead, for all your saying.

LADY MACDUFF. Yes, he is dead. How wilt thou do for a
    father?

SON. Nay, how will you do for a husband?

LADY MACDUFF. Why, I can buy me twenty at any
    market.

SON. Then you'll buy 'em to sell again.

47   **swears and lies**   vows (swears) allegiance and then breaks his oath or promise.

55   **enow**   enough.

64   **in your state . . . perfect**   I am well acquainted with your honorable condition (that you are a noblewoman).

65   **doubt**   fear.

66   **homely**   plain.

LADY MACDUFF.   Thou speak'st with all thy wit, and yet,
  i' faith,
With wit enough for thee.

SON.   Was my father a traitor, Mother?

LADY MACDUFF.   Ay, that he was.

SON.   What is a traitor?

LADY MACDUFF.   Why, one that swears and lies.   47

SON.   And be all traitors that do so?

LADY MACDUFF.   Every one that does so is a traitor, and
  must be hanged.

SON.   And must they all be hanged that swear and lie?

LADY MACDUFF.   Every one.

SON.   Who must hang them?

LADY MACDUFF.   Why, the honest men.

SON.   Then the liars and swearers are fools, for there
  are liars and swearers enow to beat the honest men   55
  and hang up them.

LADY MACDUFF.   Now, God help thee, poor monkey!
  But how wilt thou do for a father?

SON.   If he were dead, you'd weep for him; if you would
  not, it were a good sign that I should quickly have a
  new father.

LADY MACDUFF.   Poor prattler, how thou talk'st!

Enter a MESSENGER.

MESSENGER.   Bless you, fair dame! I am not to you
  known,
Though in your state of honor I am perfect.   64
I doubt some danger does approach you nearly.   65
If you will take a homely man's advice,   66
Be not found here. Hence, with your little ones!
To fright you thus, methinks I am too savage;
To do worse to you were fell cruelty,

70   **Which . . . person**   which (cruelty) is all too near at hand.

82   **fry**   offspring.

Which is too nigh your person. Heaven preserve you!   70
I dare abide no longer.

Exit.

LADY MACDUFF.   Whither should I fly?
  I have done no harm. But I remember now
  I am in this earthly world, where to do harm
  Is often laudable, to do good sometime
  Accounted dangerous folly. Why then, alas,
  Do I put up that womanly defense,
  To say I have done no harm?

Enter MURDERERS.

What are these faces?

FIRST MURDERER.   Where is your husband?

LADY MACDUFF.   I hope in no place so unsanctified
  Where such as thou mayst find him.

FIRST MURDERER.   He's a traitor.

SON.   Thous liest, thou shag-haired villain!

FIRST MURDERER.   What, you egg!
He stabs him.

  Young fry of treachery!

SON.   He has killed me, Mother.   82
  Run away, I pray you!

He dies.
Exit LADY MACDUFF, crying "Murderer!"
Exeunt MURDERERS with the SON'S body.

———————————

4 **Bestride . . . birthdom** defend our native land like one who stands over (bestrides) a fallen comrade to protect him.

8 **like syllable of dolor** similar cries of grief.

14–17 **something . . . god** Malcolm is not certain of Macduff's loyalties and thinks it possible that Macduff may reap a reward by betraying him to Macbeth since it might be wise of him to do so.

19–20 **A . . . recoil . . . in an imperial charge** A virtuous man may give way to royal command just as a cannon kicks back (recoils) after a discharge.

21 **transpose** change.

SCENE 3

In England, Malcolm closely questions Macduff's loyalty, pretends that he (Malcolm) is unfit to be king, but then says that Macduff has overcome his scruples. Ross enters and tells of the deaths of all of Macduff's household. Macduff vows to revenge the murders.

England. Before KING EDWARD'S *palace.*

Enter MALCOLM *and* MACDUFF.

MALCOLM.　Let us seek out some desolate shade, and there
　Weep our sad bosoms empty.

MACDUFF.　　　　　　　　Let us rather
　Hold fast the mortal sword, and like good men
　Bestride our downfall'n birthdom. Each new morn　　　4
　New widows howl, new orphans cry, new sorrows
　Strike heaven on the face, that it resounds
　As if it felt with Scotland and yelled out
　Like syllable of dolor.

MALCOLM.　　　　　　What I believe, I'll wail;　　　8
　What know, believe; and what I can redress,
　As I shall find the time to friend, I will.
　What you have spoke, it may be so perchance.
　This tyrant, whose sole name blisters our tongues,
　Was once thought honest; you have loved him well;
　He hath not touched you yet. I am young; but something　　14
　You may deserve of him through me, and wisdom
　To offer up a weak, poor, innocent lamb
　T' appease an angry god.

MACDUFF.　I am not treacherous.

MALCOLM　　　　　　　　　But Macbeth is.
　A good and virtuous nature may recoil　　　19
　In an imperial charge. But I shall crave your pardon.
　That which you are, my thoughts cannot transpose;　　　21
　Angels are bright still, though the brightest fell.

33–34   **wear . . . affeered**   Scotland will have to bear Macbeth's rule, for his legal right to the throne is affirmed.

43   **England**   the king of England.

Though all things foul would wear the brows of grace,
Yet grace must still look so.

MACDUFF.   I have lost my hopes.

MALCOLM.   Perchance even there where I did find my
    doubts.
Why in that rawness left you wife and child,
Those precious motives, those strong knots of love,
Without leave-taking? I pray you,
Let not my jealousies be your dishonors,
But mine own safeties. You may be rightly just,
Whatever I shall think.

MACDUFF.   Bleed, bleed, poor country!
Great tyranny, lay thou thy basis sure,
For goodness dare not check thee; wear thou thy
    wrongs,   33
The title is affeered. Fare thee well, lord.
I would not be the villain that thou think'st
For the whole space that's in the tyrant's grasp,
And the rich East to boot.

MALCOLM.   Be not offended.
I speak not as in absolute fear of you.
I think our country sinks beneath the yoke;
It weeps, it bleeds, and each new day a gash
Is added to her wounds. I think withal
There would be hands uplifted in my right;
And here from gracious England have I offer   43
Of goodly thousands. But, for all this,
When I shall tread upon the tyrant's head,
Or wear it on my sword, yet my poor country
Shall have more vices than it had before,
More suffer, and more sundry ways than ever,
By him that shall succeed.

MACDUFF.   What should he be?

MALCOLM.   It is myself I mean, in whom I know
All the particulars of vice so grafted
That, when they shall be opened, black Macbeth

141

58   **Luxurious** lecherous.

59   **sudden** violent.

78   **avarice** greed.

Will seem as pure as snow, and the poor state
Esteem him as a lamb, being compared
With my confineless harms.

MACDUFF.   Not in the legions
Of horrid hell can come a devil more damned
In evils to top Macbeth.

MALCOLM.   I grant him bloody,
Luxurious, avaricious, false, deceitful,   58
Sudden, malicious, smacking of every sin   59
That has a name. But there's no bottom, none,
In my voluptuousness. Your wives, your daughters,
Your matrons, and your maids, could not fill up
The cistern of my lust, and my desire
All continent impediments would o'erbear,
That did oppose my will. Better Macbeth
Than such an one to reign.

MACDUFF.   Boundless intemperance
In nature is a tyranny; it hath been
Th' untimely emptying of the happy throne,
And fall of many kings. But fear not yet
To take upon you what is yours. You may
Convey your pleasures in a spacious plenty,
And yet seem cold; the time you may so hoodwink.
We have willing dames enough. There cannot be
That vulture in you, to devour so many
As will to greatness dedicate themselves,
Finding it so inclined.

MALCOLM.   With this there grows
In my most ill-composed affection such
A stanchless avarice that, were I king,   78
I should cut off the nobles for their lands,
Desire his jewels and this other's house,
And my more-having would be as a sauce
To make me hunger more, that I should forge
Quarrels unjust against the good and loyal,
Destroying them for wealth.

88   **foisons** abundance.

89–90   **portable . . . weighed**   These are bearable when balanced
            against your virtues.

106   **truest issue**   that is, Malcolm.

110–111 **Oft'ner . . . lived**   Malcolm's mother prayed often, and
            through her religious life was more conscious of the next
            world than of this one.

MACDUFF. This avarice
Sticks deeper, grows with more pernicious root
Than summer-seeming lust, and it hath been
The sword of our slain kings. Yet do not fear;
Scotland hath foisons to fill up your will   88
Of your mere own. All these are portable,   89
With other graces weighed.

MALCOLM. But I have none. The king-becoming graces,
As justice, verity, temperance, stableness,
Bounty, perseverance, mercy, lowliness,
Devotion, patience, courage, fortitude,
I have no relish of them, but abound
In the division of each several crime,
Acting it many ways. Nay, had I power, I should
Pour the sweet milk of concord into hell,
Uproar the universal peace, confound
All unity on earth.

MACDUFF. O Scotland, Scotland!

MALCOLM. If such a one be fit to govern, speak.
I am as I have spoken.

MACDUFF. Fit to govern!
No, not to live. O nation miserable,
With an untitled tyrant bloody-sceptered,
When shalt thou see thy wholesome days again,
Since that the truest issue of thy throne   106
By his own interdiction stands accursed
And does blaspheme his breed? Thy royal father
Was a most sainted king; the queen that bore thee,
Oft'ner upon her knees than on her feet,   110
Died every day she lived. Fare thee well!
These evils thou repeat'st upon thyself
Hath banished me from Scotland. O my breast,
Thy hope ends here!

116   **scruples**   doubts.

118   **trains**   devices.

123   **Unspeak . . . detraction**   take back the disparaging things I
        said about myself.

140   **the King**   here, Edward.

142   **stay his cure**   wait for him to cure them.

142–143 **Their malady . . . art**   Their illness defeats the efforts of
        medical science.

MALCOLM.   Macduff, this noble passion,
   Child of integrity, hath from my soul
   Wiped the black scruples, reconciled my thoughts   116
   To thy good truth and honor. Devilish Macbeth
   By many of these trains hath sought to win me   118
   Into his power, and modest wisdom plucks me
   From overcredulous haste. But God above
   Deal between thee and me! For even now
   I put myself to thy direction and
   Unspeak mine own detraction, here abjure   123
   The taints and blames I laid upon myself
   For strangers to my nature. I am yet
   Unknown to woman, never was forsworn,
   Scarcely have coveted what was mine own,
   At no time broke my faith, would not betray
   The devil to his fellow, and delight
   No less in truth than life. My first false speaking
   Was this upon myself. What I am truly
   Is thine and my poor country's to command:
   Whither indeed, before thy here-approach,
   Old Siward, with ten thousand warlike men,
   Already at a point, was setting forth.
   Now we'll together, and the chance of goodness
   Be like our warranted quarrel! Why are you silent?

MACDUFF.   Such welcome and unwelcome things at
   once
   'Tis hard to reconcile.

Enter a DOCTOR.

MALCOLM.   Well, more anon. Comes the King forth, I
   pray you?   140

DOCTOR.   Ay, sir. There are a crew of wretched souls
   That stay his cure. Their malady convinces   142
   The great assay of art; but at his touch,
   Such sanctity hath heaven given his hand,
   They presently amend.

145   **presently amend**   are immediately healed.

146   **the evil**   scrofula, a disease of the lymph glands,
        sometimes called the king's evil because it was thought to
        be cured by a king's touch. This passage was probably
        included to honor James I, who continued the practice
        begun by Edward the Confessor of touching scrofula
        victims.

153   **stamp**   coin.

160   **My countryman . . . not**   Malcolm recognizes Ross as
        Scottish by his clothing. That he has forgotten exactly who
        Ross is may indicate that Malcolm has been in England for
        some time.

MALCOLM.   I thank you, Doctor.   145

                          Exit DOCTOR.

MACDUFF.   What's the disease he means?

MALCOLM.   'Tis called the evil.   146
   A most miraculous work in this good king;
   Which often, since my here-remain in England,
   I have seen him do. How he solicits heaven
   Himself best knows; but strangely-visited people,
   All swoll'n and ulcerous, pitiful to the eye,
   The mere despair of surgery, he cures,
   Hanging a golden stamp about their necks,   153
   Put on with holy prayers; and 'tis spoken,
   To the succeeding royalty he leaves
   The healing benediction. With this strange virtue
   He hath a heavenly gift of prophecy,
   And sundry blessings hang about his throne
   That speak him full of grace.

                 Enter ROSS.

MACDUFF.   See who comes here.

MALCOLM.   My countryman; but yet I know him not.   160

MACDUFF.   My ever-gentle cousin, welcome hither.

MALCOLM.   I know him now. Good God betimes remove
   The means that makes us strangers!

ROSS.   Sir, amen.

MACDUFF.   Stands Scotland where it did?

ROSS.   Alas, poor country,
   Almost afraid to know itself! It cannot
   Be called our mother, but our grave; where nothing,
   But who knows nothing, is once seen to smile;
   Where sighs and groans and shrieks that rend the air,

174   **nice**   minutely accurate.

180   **a niggard**   stingy person.

183   **out**   in the field (in arms against Macbeth).

184–185 **Which was . . . afoot**   My belief was confirmed because I saw Macbeth's army on the march.

Are made, not marked; where violent sorrow seems
A modern ecstasy. The dead man's knell
Is there scarce asked for who; and good men's lives
Expire before the flowers in their caps,
Dying or ere they sicken.

MACDUFF.   O, relation
  Too nice, and yet too true!

MALCOLM.   What's the newest grief?   174

ROSS.   That of an hour's age doth hiss the speaker;
  Each minute teems a new one.

MACDUFF   How does my wife?

ROSS.   Why, well.

MACDUFF.   And all my children?

ROSS.   Well too.

MACDUFF.   The tyrant has not battered at their peace?

ROSS.   No; they were well at peace when I did leave
      'em.

MACDUFF.   Be not a niggard of your speech. How goes 't?   180

ROSS.   When I came hither to transport the tidings
  Which I have heavily borne, there ran a rumor
  Of many worthy fellows that were out,   183
  Which was to my belief witnessed the rather   184
  For that I saw the tyrant's power afoot.
  Now is the time of help; your eye in Scotland
  Would create soldiers, make our women fight,
  To doff their dire distresses.

MALCOLM.   Be 't their comfort
  We are coming thither. Gracious England hath
  Lent us good Siward and ten thousand men;
  An older and a better soldier none
  That Christendom gives out.

195   **latch**   catch the sound of.

196   **fee-grief**   a private grief.

203   **Hum!**   probably a groan.

ROSS. Would I could answer
This comfort with the like! But I have words
That would be howled out in the desert air,
Where hearing should not latch them.

MACDUFF. What concern they? 195
The general cause? Or is it a fee-grief 196
Due to some single breast?

ROSS. No mind that's honest
But in it shares some woe, though the main part
Pertains to you alone.

MACDUFF. If it be mine,
Keep it not from me; quickly let me have it.

ROSS. Let not your ears despise my tongue forever,
Which shall possess them with the heaviest sound
That ever yet they heard.

MACDUFF. Hum! I guess at it. 203

ROSS. Your castle is surprised; your wife and babes
Savagely slaughtered: To relate the manner,
Were, on the quarry of these murdered deer,
To add the death of you.

MALCOLM. Merciful heaven!
What, man, ne'er pull your hat upon your brows;
Give sorrow words. The grief that does not speak
Whispers the o'erfraught heart and bids it break.

MACDUFF. My children too?

ROSS. Wife, children, servants, all
That could be found.

MACDUFF. And I must be from thence!
My wife killed too?

ROSS. I have said.

MALCOLM. Be comforted.
Let's make us medicines of our great revenge
To cure this deadly grief.

216 **He has no children**   This line has been interpreted in several ways. Macduff may be speaking of Malcolm, who cannot know the grief of a father, or of Macbeth, who would not have murdered children had he any of his own.

237 **Our . . . leave**   We need only to take our leave [of Edward].

MACDUFF.   He has no children. All my pretty ones?   216
    Did you say all? O hell-kite! All?
    What, all my pretty chickens and their dam
    At one fell swoop?

MALCOLM.   Dispute it like a man.

MACDUFF.   I shall do so;
    But I must also feel it as a man.
    I cannot but remember such things were,
    That were most precious to me. Did heaven look on
    And would not take their part? Sinful Macduff,
    They were all struck for thee! Naught that I am,
    Not for their own demerits, but for mine,
    Fell slaughter on their souls. Heaven rest them now!

MALCOLM.   Be this the whetstone of your sword. Let
        grief
    Convert to anger; blunt not the heart, enrage it.

MACDUFF.   O, I could play the woman with mine eyes
    And braggart with my tongue! But, gentle heavens,
    Cut short all intermission. Front to front
    Bring thou this fiend of Scotland and myself;
    Within my sword's length set him; if he scape,
    Heaven forgive him too!

MALCOLM.   This tune goes manly.
    Come, go we to the King. Our power is ready;
    Our lack is nothing but our leave. Macbeth   237
    Is ripe for shaking, and the powers above
    Put on their instruments. Receive what cheer you
        may.
    The night is long that never finds the day.
                                        Exeunt.

MACBETH

ACT V

"More needs she the divine than the physician."

6 **closet** chest or desk.

17 **meet** proper.

SCENE 1

A doctor and a gentlewoman discuss Lady Macbeth's affliction. Lady Macbeth, walking in her sleep, speaks of her feelings of guilt.

Dunsinane. Macbeth's castle.

Enter a DOCTOR OF PHYSIC *and a*
WAITING-GENTLEWOMAN.

DOCTOR. I have two nights watched with you, but can perceive no truth in your report. When was it she last walked?

GENTLEWOMAN. Since his Majesty went into the field, I have seen her rise from her bed, throw her nightgown upon her, unlock her closet, take forth paper, fold it, write upon 't, read it, afterwards seal it, and again return to bed; yet all this while in a most fast sleep.

6

DOCTOR. A great perturbation in nature, to receive at once the benefit of sleep and do the effects of watching! In this slumbery agitation, besides her walking and other actual performances, what, at any time, have your heard her say?

GENTLEWOMAN. That, sir, which I will not report after her.

DOCTOR. You may to me, and 'tis most meet you should.

17

GENTLEWOMAN. Neither to you nor any one, having no witness to confirm my speech.

Enter LADY MACBETH, *with a taper.*
Lo you, here she comes! This is her very guise, and, upon my life, fast asleep. Observe her; stand close.

DOCTOR. How came she by that light?

GENTLEWOMAN. Why, it stood by her. She has light by her continually. 'Tis her command.

47   **starting**   startled movements.

56–57   **sorely charged**   heavily burdened.

DOCTOR.   You see her eyes are open.

GENTLEWOMAN.   Ay, but their sense are shut.

DOCTOR.   What is it she does now? Look how she rubs her hands.

GENTLEWOMAN.   It is an accustomed action with her, to seem thus washing her hands. I have known her continue in this a quarter of an hour.

LADY MACBETH.   Yet here's a spot.

DOCTOR.   Hark, she speaks. I will set down what comes from her, to satisfy my remembrance the more strongly.

LADY MACBETH.   Out, damned spot! Out, I say! One; two. Why then 'tis time to do 't. Hell is murky. Fie, my lord, fie! A soldier, and afeard? What need we fear who knows it, when none can call our power to account? Yet who would have thought the old man to have had so much blood in him?

DOCTOR.   Do you mark that?

LADY MACBETH.   The Thane of Fife had a wife. Where is she now? What, will these hands ne'er be clean? No more o' that, my lord, no more o' that; you mar all with this starting.   47

DOCTOR.   Go to, go to. You have known what you should not.

GENTLEWOMAN.   She has spoke what she should not, I am sure of that. Heaven knows what she has known.

LADY MACBETH.   Here's the smell of the blood still. All the perfumes of Arabia will not sweeten this little hand. Oh, oh, oh!

DOCTOR.   What a sigh is there! The heart is sorely   56
charged.

GENTLEWOMAN.   I would not have such a heart in my bosom for the dignity of the whole body.

80   **annoyance**   injury to herself.

82   **mated**   stupefied.

DOCTOR.   Well, well, well.

GENTLEWOMAN.   Pray God it be, sir.

DOCTOR.   This disease is beyond my practice. Yet I
have known those which have walked in their sleep
who have died holily in their beds.

LADY MACBETH.   Wash your hands, put on your
nightgown, look not so pale! I tell you yet again,
Banquo's buried. He cannot come out on 's grave.

DOCTOR.   Even so?

LADY MACBETH.   To bed, to bed! There's knocking at
the gate. Come, come, come, come, give me your
hand. What's done cannot be undone. To bed, to
bed, to bed.

Exit.

DOCTOR.   Will she go now to bed?

GENTLEWOMAN.   Directly.

DOCTOR.   Foul whisperings are abroad. Unnatural deeds
Do breed unnatural troubles. Infected minds
To their deaf pillows will discharge their secrets.
More needs she the divine than the physician.
God, God forgive us all! Look after her;
Remove from her the means of all annoyance,   80
And still keep eyes upon her. So good night.
My mind she has mated, and amazed my sight.   82
I think, but dare not speak.

GENTLEWOMAN.   Good night, good doctor.

Exeunt.

163

3   **dear** heartfelt.

5   **Excite the mortified man** rouse the dead.

11   **Protest their first of manhood** show for the first time that they are men because this is their first battle.

18   **Now minutely . . . faith-breach** Now, every minute, rebellions reproach him for his treachery.

SCENE 2

Angus, Lennox, and others discuss the coming battle against Macbeth's forces at Dunsinane.

The country near Dunsinane.

Drum and colors. Enter MENTEITH, CAITHNESS,
ANGUS, LENNOX, SOLDIERS.

MENTEITH. The English power is near, led on by
   Malcolm,
   His uncle Siward, and the good Macduff.
   Revenges burn in them, for their dear causes   3
   Would to the bleeding and the grim alarm
   Excite the mortified man.

ANGUS.   Near Birnam Wood   5
   Shall we well meet them; that way are they coming.

CAITHNESS. Who knows if Donalbain be with his
   brother?

LENNOX. For certain, sir, he is not. I have a file
   Of all the gentry. There is Siward's son,
   And many unrough youths, that even now
   Protest their first of manhood.

MENTEITH.   What does the tyrant?   11

CAITHNESS. Great Dunsinane he strongly fortifies.
   Some say he's mad; others, that lesser hate him,
   Do call it valiant fury; but for certain
   He cannot buckle his distempered cause
   Within the belt of rule.

ANGUS   Now does he feel
   His secret murders sticking on his hands;
   Now minutely revolts upbraid his faith-breach.   18
   Those he commands move only in command,
   Nothing in love. Now does he feel his title
   Hang loose about him, like a giant's robe
   Upon a dwarfish thief.

165

23   **pestered** troubled.

27–29   **Meet we . . . purge . . . us** a medical metaphor. Let us join
         Malcolm, the healer of our sick nation, and shed our blood
         in order to rid the country of its illness.

3   **taint** become infected.

8   **epicures** luxury-loving people.

MENTEITH.   Who then shall blame
  His pestered senses to recoil and start,   23
  When all that is within him does condemn
  Itself for being there?

CAITHNESS.   Well, march we on
  To give obedience where 'tis truly owed.
  Meet we the med'cine of the sickly weal,   27
  And with him pour we in our country's purge,
  Each drop of us.

LENNOX.   Or so much as it needs
  To dew the sovereign flower and drown the weeds.
  Make we our march towards Birnam.

                                  Exeunt, marching.

SCENE 3

Macbeth asks the doctor for reports of Lady Macbeth. He then discovers from a
servant that the English forces are near and gets ready for battle.

Dunsinane. A room in the castle.

Enter MACBETH, DOCTOR, *and* ATTENDANTS.

MACBETH.   Bring me no more reports. Let them fly all!
  Till Birnam Wood remove to Dunsinane
  I cannot taint with fear. What's the boy Malcolm?   3
  Was he not born of woman? The spirits that know
  All mortal consequences have pronounced me thus:
  "Fear not, Macbeth. No man that's born of woman
  Shall e'er have power upon thee." Then fly, false
    thanes,
  And mingle with the English epicures.   8

15   **patch** fool.

24   **sere** dry and withered.

The mind I sway by and the heart I bear
Shall never sag with doubt nor shake with fear.

Enter SERVANT.

The devil damn thee black, thou cream-faced loon!
Where gott'st thou that goose look?

SERVANT.   There is ten thousand—

MACBETH.   Geese, villain?

SERVANT.   Soldiers, sir.

MACBETH.   Go prick thy face and over-red thy fear,
Thou lily-livered boy. What soldiers, patch!   15
Death of my soul! Those linen cheeks of thine
Are counselors to fear. What soldiers, whey-face?

SERVANT.   The English force, so please you.

MACBETH.   Take thy face hence.

Exit SERVANT.

Seyton!—I am sick at heart,
When I behold—Seyton, I say!—This push
Will cheer me ever, or disseat me now.
I have lived long enough. My way of life
Is fall'n into the sere, the yellow leaf,   24
And that which should accompany old age,
As honor, love, obedience, troops of friends,
I must not look to have but, in their stead,
Curses, not loud but deep, mouth-honor, breath,
Which the poor heart would fain deny and dare not.
Seyton!

Enter SEYTON.

SEYTON.   What's your gracious pleasure?

MACBETH.   What news more?

SEYTON.   All is confirmed, my lord, which was reported.

36   **Skirr**   scour.

43   **Raze**   erase.

55   **Pull 't off**   a reference to some part of his armor, which Seyton is trying to help him with.

MACBETH.   I'll fight till from my bones my flesh be
    hacked.
Give me my armor.

SEYTON.   'Tis not needed yet.

MACBETH.   I'll put it on.
    Send out more horses. Skirr the country round.   36
    Hang those that talk of fear. Give me mine armor.
    How does your patient, Doctor?

DOCTOR.   Not so sick, my lord,
    As she is troubled with thick-coming fancies
    That keep her from her rest.

MACBETH.   Cure her of that.
    Canst thou not minister to a mind diseased,
    Pluck from the memory a rooted sorrow,
    Raze out the written troubles of the brain,   43
    And with some sweet oblivious antidote
    Cleanse the stuffed bosom of that perilous stuff
    Which weighs upon the heart?

DOCTOR.   Therein the patient
    Must minister to himself.

MACBETH.   Throw physic to the dogs! I'll none of it.
    Come, put mine armor on. Give me my staff.
    Seyton, send out. Doctor, the thanes fly from me.—
    Come, sir, dispatch.—If thou couldst, Doctor, cast
    The water of my land, find her disease,
    And purge it to a sound and pristine health,
    I would applaud thee to the very echo,
    That should applaud again.—Pull 't off, I say.—   55
    What rhubarb, senna, or what purgative drug,
    Would scour these English hence? Hear'st thou of
    them?

DOCTOR.   Ay, my good lord. Your royal preparation
    Makes us hear something.

5–6   **shadow . . . host**   conceal how many of us there are.

6   **discovery**   scouting reports.

MACBETH.   Bring it after me.—
I will not be afraid of death and bane,
Till Birnam Forest come to Dunsinane.

Exeunt all but DOCTOR.

DOCTOR.   Were I from Dunsinane away and clear,
Profit again should hardly draw me here.

Exit.

SCENE 4

Near Birnam Wood, the English troops disguise themselves with branches from the forest.

Country near Birnam Wood.

Drum and colors. Enter MALCOLM, SIWARD,
MACDUFF, SIWARD'S SON, MENTEITH, CAITHNESS,
ANGUS, LENNOX, ROSS, *and* SOLDIERS, *marching.*

MALCOLM.   Cousins, I hope the days are near at hand
That chambers will be safe.

MENTEITH.   We doubt it nothing.

SIWARD.   What wood is this before us?

MENTEITH.   The wood of Birnam.

MALCOLM.   Let every soldier hew him down a bough,
And bear 't before him. Thereby shall we shadow   5
The numbers of our host and make discovery   6
Err in report of us.

SOLDIERS.   It shall be done.

18   **owe**   own.

19–20   **Thoughts speculative . . . arbitrate**   Guesses only tell of
our hopes, but blows (strokes) must decide the battle's
outcome.

SIWARD.   We learn no other but the confident tyrant
Keeps still in Dunsinane and will endure
Our setting down before 't.

MALCOLM.   'Tis his main hope;
For where there is advantage to be given,
Both more and less have given him the revolt,
And none serve with him but constrainèd things
Whose hearts are absent too.

MACDUFF.   Let our just censures
Attend the true event, and put we on
Industrious soldiership.

SIWARD.   The time approaches
That will with due decision make us know
What we shall say we have and what we owe.   18
Thoughts speculative their unsure hopes relate,   19
But certain issue strokes must arbitrate —
Towards which advance the war.

                              Exeunt, marching.

SCENE 5

*Macbeth learns that Lady Macbeth is dead and that Birnam Wood
approaches. He prepares to fight.*

Dunsinane. Within the castle.

Enter MACBETH, SEYTON, *and* SOLDIERS, *with drum
and colors.*

MACBETH.   Hang out our banners on the outward walls.
The cry is still "They come!" Our castle's strength
Will laugh a seige to scorn. Here let them lie
Till famine and the ague eat them up.

5   **forced**   reinforced.

6   **dareful**   boldly.

12   **treatise**   story.

17   **She . . . hereafter**   She would have died sometime, *or* she should have died at another, perhaps more peaceful, time.

Were they not forced with those that should be ours,   5
We might have met them dareful, beard to beard,   6
And beat them backward home.

                  A cry within of women.
                What is that noise?
                        Exit.

SEYTON.   It is the cry of women, my good lord.

MACBETH.   I have almost forgot the taste of fears.
   The time has been, my senses would have cooled
   To hear a night-shriek, and my fell of hair
   Would at a dismal treatise rouse and stir   12
   As life were in 't. I have supped full with horrors;
   Direness, familiar to my slaughterous thoughts,
   Cannot once start me.

                Enter SEYTON.
                Wherefore was that cry?

SEYTON.   The Queen, my lord, is dead.

MACBETH.   She should have died hereafter;   17
   There would have been a time for such a word.
   Tomorrow, and tomorrow, and tomorrow
   Creeps in this petty pace from day to day
   To the last syllable of recorded time,
   And all our yesterdays have lighted fools
   The way to dusty death. Out, out, brief candle!
   Life's but a walking shadow, a poor player
   That struts and frets his hour upon the stage
   And then is heard no more. It is a tale
   Told by an idiot, full of sound and fury,
   Signifying nothing.

              Enter a MESSENGER.
Thou comest to use thy tongue; thy story quickly.

MESSENGER.   Gracious my lord,
   I should report that which I say I saw,
   But know not how to do 't.

MACBETH.   Well, say, sir.

40   **sooth**   truth.

42   **pull in**   rein in.

47   **avouches**   affirms.

MESSENGER.   As I did stand my watch upon the hill,
  I looked toward Birnam, and anon, methought,
  The wood began to move.

MACBETH.   Liar and slave!

MESSENGER.   Let me endure your wrath, if 't be not so.
  Within this three mile may you see it coming;
  I say, a moving grove.

MACBETH.   If thou speak'st false,
  Upon the next tree shalt thou hang alive
  Till famine cling thee. If thy speech be sooth,   40
  I care not if thou dost for me as much.
  I pull in resolution, and begin   42
  To doubt th' equivocation of the fiend
  That lies like truth. "Fear not, till Birnam Wood
  Do come to Dunsinane," and now a wood
  Comes toward Dunsinane. Arm, arm, and out!
  If this which he avouches does appear,   47
  There is nor flying hence nor tarrying here.
  I 'gin to be aweary of the sun,
  And wish th' estate o' the world were now undone.
  Ring the alarum bell! Blow wind, come wrack,
  At least we'll die with harness on our back.
                                        Exeunt.

SCENE 6

Malcolm gives orders as his forces prepare to lay siege to the castle.

Dunsinane. Before the castle.
Drum and colors. Enter MALCOLM, SIWARD,
  MACDUFF, *and their army, with boughs.*

6   **order**   battle plan.

1–2   **They . . . course**   Macbeth is comparing himself to a bear in the "sport" of bearbaiting, who was tied to a stake, attacked by dogs, and had to endure several bouts (courses).

MALCOLM.   Now near enough. Your leafy screens throw
    down,
    And show like those you are. You, worthy uncle,
    Shall with my cousin, your right noble son,
    Lead our first battle. Worthy Macduff and we
    Shall take upon 's what else remains to do,
    According to our order.   6

SIWARD.   Fare you well.
    Do we but find the tyrant's power tonight,
    Let us be beaten if we cannot fight.

MACDUFF.   Make all our trumpets speak; give them all
    breath,
    Those clamorous harbingers of blood and death.
                           Exeunt. Alarums continued.

SCENE 7

Macbeth kills Young Siward. Macduff approaches.

Another part of the field.

Enter MACBETH.

MACBETH.   They have tied me to a stake. I cannot fly,   1
    But bearlike I must fight the course. What's he
    That was not born of woman? Such a one
    Am I to fear, or none.

Enter YOUNG SIWARD.

YOUNG SIWARD.   What is thy name?

MACBETH.   Thou'lt be afraid to hear it.

21–22   **By this . . . bruited**   The noise seems to indicate that
Macbeth is near.

24   **rendered**   surrendered.

YOUNG SIWARD.   No; though thou call'st thyself a
     hotter name
Than any is in hell.

MACBETH.   My name's Macbeth.

YOUNG SIWARD.   The devil himself could not
     pronounce a title
More hateful to mine ear.

MACBETH.   No, nor more fearful.

YOUNG SIWARD.   Thou liest, abhorrèd tyrant! With my
     sword
I'll prove the lie thou speak'st.
                    They fight, and YOUNG SIWARD *is slain.*

MACBETH.   Thou wast born of woman.
But swords I smile at, weapons laugh to scorn,
Brandished by man that's of a woman born.
                                        Exit.

                    Alarums. Enter MACDUFF.

MACDUFF.   That way the noise is. Tyrant, show thy
     face!
If thou be'st slain and with no stroke of mine,
My wife and children's ghosts will haunt me still.
I cannot strike at wretched kerns, whose arms
Are hired to bear their staves. Either thou, Macbeth,
Or else my sword with an unbattered edge
I sheathe again undeeded. There thou shouldst be;
By this great clatter one of greatest note   21
Seems bruited. Let me find him, Fortune!
And more I beg not.
                              Exit. Alarums.

                    Enter MALCOLM *and* SIWARD.

SIWARD.   This way, my lord. The castle's gently
     rendered: 24
The tyrant's people on both sides do fight,

183

1   **play the Roman fool**   commit suicide, as Roman officials did to avoid capture.

2   **lives**   living enemies.

9   **intrenchant**   incapable of being penetrated or cut.

The noble thanes do bravely in the war,
The day almost itself professes yours,
And little is to do.

MALCOLM.   We have met with foes
    That strike besides us.

SIWARD.   Enter, sir, the castle.

> *Exeunt. Alarum.*

SCENE 8

*Macbeth and Macduff fight, and Macbeth is killed and beheaded.
Malcolm is hailed as king.*

Dunsinane. In front of the castle.

Enter MACBETH.

MACBETH.   Why should I play the Roman fool and die   1
    On mine own sword? Whiles I see lives, the gashes   2
    Do better upon them.

Enter MACDUFF.

MACDUFF.   Turn, hellhound, turn!

MACBETH.   Of all men else I have avoided thee.
    But get thee back. My soul is too much charged
    With blood of thine already.

MACDUFF.   I have no words;
    My voice is in my sword, thou bloodier villain
    Than terms can give thee out!

> *Fight. Alarum.*

MACBETH.   Thou losest labor.
    As easy mayst thou the intrenchant air   9
    With thy keen sword impress as make me bleed.

16   **untimely ripped**   born prematurely, probably by Caesarean section.

19   **juggling**   deceiving.

20   **palter**   trifle; deal crookedly.

36   **go off**   die; **by**   judging by.

Let fall thy blade on vulnerable crests;
I bear a charmèd life, which must not yield
To one of woman born.
MACDUFF.   Despair thy charm,
    And let the angel whom thou still hast served
    Tell thee, Macduff was from his mother's womb
    Untimely ripped.   16

MACBETH.   Accursèd be that tongue that tells me so,
    For it hath cowed my better part of man!
    And be these juggling fiends no more believed,   19
    That palter with us in a double sense,   20
    That keep the word of promise to our ear,
    And break it to our hope. I'll not fight with thee.

MACDUFF.   Then yield thee, coward,
    And live to be the show and gaze o' the time!
    We'll have thee, as our rarer monsters are,
    Painted upon a pole, and underwrit,
    "Here may you see the tyrant."

MACBETH.   I will not yield,
    To kiss the ground before young Malcolm's feet
    And to be baited with the rabble's curse.
    Though Birnam Wood be come to Dunsinane,
    And thou opposed, being of no woman born,
    Yet I will try the last. Before my body
    I throw my warlike shield. Lay on, Macduff,
    And damned be him that first cries "Hold, enough!"
                                        Exeunt, fighting.

            Enter, fighting, and MACBETH *is slain.*
            Exit MACDUFF *with* MACBETH'S *body.*
    Retreat, and flourish. Enter, with drum and colors,
                MALCOLM, SIWARD, ROSS,
                THANES, *and* SOLDIERS.
MALCOLM.   I would the friends we miss were safe
    arrived.

SIWARD.   Some must go off; and yet, by these I see   36
    So great a day as this is cheaply bought.

50   **knell is knolled**   funeral bell is rung.

56   **compassed . . . pearl**   surrounded by your nobles.

MALCOLM.   Macduff is missing, and your noble son.

ROSS.   Your son, my lord, has paid a soldier's debt.
He only lived but till he was a man,
The which no sooner had his prowess confirmed
In the unshrinking station where he fought,
But like a man he died.

SIWARD.   Then he is dead?

ROSS.   Ay, and brought off the field. Your cause of
    sorrow
Must not be measured by his worth, for then
It hath no end.

SIWARD.   Had he his hurts before?

ROSS.   Ay, on the front.

SIWARD.   Why then, God's soldier be he!
Had I as many sons as I have hairs,
I would not wish them to a fairer death.
And so his knell is knolled.

MALCOLM.   He's worth more sorrow,   50
And that I'll spend for him.

SIWARD.   He's worth no more.
They say he parted well and paid his score,
And so God be with him! Here comes newer comfort.

Enter MACDUFF, *with* MACBETH'S *head.*

MACDUFF.   Hail, King! For so thou art. Behold where
    stands
The usurper's cursèd head. The time is free.
I see thee compassed with thy kingdom's pearl,   56
That speak my salutation in their minds,
Whose voices I desire aloud with mine:
Hail, King of Scotland!

ALL.   Hail, King of Scotland!
                                             Flourish.

189

62   **make . . . you** repay your worthiness.

65   **would . . . time** should be established at the beginning of this new era.

MALCOLM.   We shall not spend a large expense of time
    Before we reckon with your several loves
    And make us even with you. My thanes and kinsmen,   62
    Henceforth be earls, the first that ever Scotland
    In such an honor named. What's more to do
    Which would be planted newly with the time,   65
    As calling home our exiled friends abroad
    That fled the snares of watchful tyranny,
    Producing forth the cruel ministers
    Of this dead butcher and his fiendlike queen,
    Who, as 'tis thought, by self and violent hands
    Took off her life; this, and what needful else
    That calls upon us, by the grace of Grace
    We will perform in measure, time, and place.
    So thanks to all at once and to each one,
    Whom we invite to see us crowned at Scone.

                    Flourish. Exeunt omnes.

Thinking About the Play

Act I

1. What do the witches know about Macbeth, and what do they prophesy for him and for Banquo?

2. What troubles Macbeth the most throughout Act I?

3. How does Lady Macbeth attempt to influence Macbeth, and what are his reactions?

4. *Dramatic irony* occurs when the reader or audience is aware of events unknown to one or more characters. Its purpose is to create tension and suspense. What are some instances of dramatic irony in Act I?

5. Which characters, other than Duncan, also may be in danger? Why?

Act II

1. Reread the part of Scene 1 in which Macbeth sees the dagger. This scene has been depicted in film and on the stage in several ways. In some productions, an actual dagger has been suspended by wires. Often the dagger is "visible" only to Macbeth, imagined by the audience but not actually present. Projected and shifting shadows, which may or may not indicate a dagger, have been effective. Consider the nature of the play so far, as well as the intended effect of the scene. As a director, how

would you stage this scene for maximum effect in a live performance? Be ready to back up your decision in class discussion.

2. At the beginning of Scene 2, what is Lady Macbeth's excuse for not committing the crime herself? Is this in keeping with her "undaunted mettle" in Act I, or is she beginning to change?

3. Two things trouble Macbeth immediately after the murder. What are they, and what might they mean for his future?

4. The drunken Porter's scene has at least two purposes. What are they?

5. After the discovery of the murder, Macbeth's speech, beginning "Had I but died before . . . ." (Scene 3, lines 92–97), might mean one thing to Banquo, Macduff, Lennox, and Ross, and quite another to Macbeth himself. Explain how this speech can be understood in two ways.

6. In Scene 3, in response to Macduff's question, Macbeth tells why he killed the grooms beginning with "Who can be wise . . . ." (lines 110–120). What do you think of this speech? Is it effective? Convincing? Eloquent? True?

Act III

1. In Scene 1, Macbeth refers to his "fruitless crown" and "barren scepter." Why does he use these adjectives?

2. What is Macbeth's state of mind in Scene 2, lines 13–26, beginning with "We have scorched the snake . . . ."?

3. For a live production, how would you stage the scene in which Banquo's ghost appears? Which alternative—having the ghost appear or having an empty seat—would appeal most to an audience? Which would best convey the intended effect of the scene?

4. How has the nature of the relationship between Macbeth and Lady Macbeth changed in this act?

5. At the end of Scene 4, Macbeth vows to send for Macduff. Where has Macduff gone, and of what might Macbeth suspect Macduff?

Act IV

1. What does Macbeth learn about himself when he consults the witches?
2. In some early productions of the play, the scene with Lady Macduff and her son was omitted. What, in your opinion, was Shakespeare's purpose in including this scene?
3. What is the general condition of Scotland by this time?
4. What is Malcolm's method for testing Macduff's true feelings about Macbeth?
5. What has been resolved between Macduff and Malcolm at the end of Act IV?

Act V

1. What are some possible interpretations of Lady Macbeth's behavior in Scene 1?
2. What is Macbeth's state of mind in Scenes 3 and 5?
3. In Scene 2 Angus says that Macbeth feels his title "Hang loose about him, like a giant's robe/Upon a dwarfish thief." This recalls Macbeth's remark in Act I, Scene 3: "The Thane of Cawdor lives. Why do you dress me/In borrowed robes?" It also recalls Banquo's comment that Macbeth's new honors are like garments that "cleave not to their mold," or have not yet become fitted to the wearer. What do these three metaphorical expressions reveal about Macbeth, and why might metaphors concerning clothes be appropriate in this play?
4. Macbeth at first refuses to fight Macduff, but he changes his mind. Why?
5. How do you feel about Macbeth after reading the play? What parts of the play most affected your response?

Acts I–V

1. There are frequent references to the natural world in *Macbeth*. Explore some of the possible purposes these references serve.

2. In tragedy the main character suffers defeat after a serious and major struggle. Through this defeat the character attains heroic stature. Macbeth suffers defeat, but does he attain heroic stature? Defend your answer.

3. Lady Macbeth is a tragic figure as well. What has caused her downfall? Is she weaker than Macbeth? More prone to understand the nature of sin? Has she deceived herself? Was she less able than Macbeth to foresee the consequences of her actions? Be prepared to discuss your answers in class.

4. One critic has written that Shakespeare's tragedy "wells up from a deep awareness of evil, yet it never forsakes belief in the eternal good." Do you agree with this statement? Explain your answer.

5. Does *Macbeth* have relevance for people today? If so, how? If not, why not?

Responding Through Writing

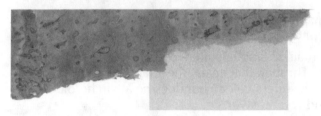

Act I

Imagine that you are a servant in the Macbeth household. Undoubtedly, in your comings and goings, you have overheard or seen a great many things. Write a letter to a friend describing what has happened since Lady Macbeth received her letter from Macbeth. Describe the nature of the relationship between Macbeth and Lady Macbeth. Remember that you have been hard at work in the castle, so you have not observed anything that has happened elsewhere.

Act II

Macbeth is distressed by the voice he thinks said "Sleep no more!" and he goes on to extol the virtues of sleep. Recall the First Witch's punishment of the sailor in Act I: "Sleep shall neither night nor day/ Hang upon his penthouse lid." In the beginning of Act II, Banquo does not wish to sleep because of "cursed thoughts that nature/ Gives way to in repose." Where else in Act II is sleep mentioned or of major significance? Make notes of these passages and of other passages about sleep as you continue the play. Be prepared to write a paper or give a talk on this motif and its meaning for the play after you have finished the last act.

Act III

The struggle between opposing forces, or *conflict*, is necessary to any plot. What are the conflicts in this play so far? Are some conflicts more important than others? Make a list of the conflicts and arrange them in order, ending with the most important. Then write an essay in which you identify and describe each conflict. Assume you are writing for someone who does not understand the play.

Act IV

In Scene 3, lines 91–94, Malcolm lists the virtues that a king should have. What, in your opinion, are the virtures that a leader *should* have? Give your answer in three to five paragraphs.

Act V

Macbeth realizes at last that the witches have deceived him. Are they responsible in any way for his fate? Is Lady Macbeth responsible? Is Macbeth himself responsible? Write a persuasive paper analyzing the reasons for Macbeth's downfall.

Acts I–V

1. Suppose that you are the artistic director for a production of *Macbeth*. Your task is to see that all the production elements— sets, lighting, costumes, props, special effects—convey a unified impression. What impression would this be?

   Write a memo to your production staff in which you explain the overall effects you wish to achieve. You need not tell your staff how to do their specific jobs. You do need to explain your artistic vision.

2. Organize the notes you have been keeping on the passages that refer to sleep. Decide why sleep is important to the play and write a paper on this motif.

3. *Macbeth* is full of deceptions and false appearances. Trace the instances of these and write a paper in which you explore how they contribute to Macbeth's downfall.

Enrichment Activities

1. Using the *Readers' Guide to Periodical Literature*, research the discovery in 1989 of the remains of the Rose Theatre in London. What have archaeologists learned about the site? Report to the class.

2. Photocopy a drawing or a photo of a hypothetical model of the Globe Theatre. Explain the various parts of the theatre to the class.

3. Research the superstitions about *Macbeth*, both in rehearsal and in performance, and make a class presentation.

4. As an investigative reporter, write a news story about the deaths of Duncan and his two servants, and about other events surrounding this mystery. Alternatively, you and other class members might produce a four-page newspaper—the *Inverness Times* or the *Dunsinane Herald*—with various news stories, columns, features, editorials, and cartoons.

5. Perform part of a scene from *Macbeth* with one or more of your classmates.

6. Design costumes or sets for a production of *Macbeth*.

7. Compose and perform a song that could serve as accompaniment to or background for one of the witches' scenes.